American Society: Upside Down

Essays on the 2016 Presidential Election

American Society: Upside Down

Essays on the 2016 Presidential Election

Bobby E. Mills, Ph.D.

American Society: Upside Down: Essays on the 2016 Presidential Election
by Bobby E. Mills, Ph.D.

© Copyright 2017

SAINT PAUL PRESS, DALLAS, TEXAS

First Printing, 2017.

ISBN-13: 978-1542515221
ISBN-10: 154251522X

Printed in the U.S.A.

CONTENTS

Acknowledgments 7

Introduction 9

1. The Donald Trump Phenomenon: Par for the Course 15

2. Make America Great Again! 19

3. Beware of Individuals With All the Answers 23

4. A Socio-Religious Viewpoint On Political Governance 27

5. Blue Collar Mentality versus White Collar Mentality 31

6. Can We All Get Along? 35

7. Can You Believe This? 39

8. Does American Society Deserve 2016
   Presidential Confusion? 43

9. Fear Can Make Individuals Say and Do Unholy Things 47

10. Godhead Leadership, Pastoral Leadership,
    and Congregational Stewardship 51

11. Gutter Rat Politics 55

12. If You Talk the Talk You Should Walk the Walk 59

13. Is Life Too Cheap? 63

14. Knowledge and IQ In a Social Democracy 67

15. The Missing Moral Links 71

16. One in God, and All in Christ 75

17. Partisan Politics: Public Policy 79

18. Politics and Strange Bed Partners 83

19. Religious Conservatism versus All White Conservatism 87

20. Don't Sell Out the American Dream 91

21. The Aftermath: A Nation Divided 95

22. The Hoodwinking of Working Class White Males 99

23. The System 103

24. The Tyranny of the Majority 107

25. The Welfare System 111

26. Unqualified 115

27. American Society: Upside-Down and Under-Water 119

28. What In the "Hell" Do You Have to Lose? 123

29. What's Going On? 127

30. Whom Do You Love More: Creator Or Creation? 133

31. Why Blacks And Whites Do Not Worship Together 135

32. America's National Security Disaster 139

33. Words and Elections Have Consequences 143

Conclusion 141

ACKNOWLEDGMENTS

The 2016 presidential election flipped American society upside down and inside out and placed it under water. In fact, American society is spiritually and morally topsy-turvy. In 2016, Americans were given a bilateral choice for President, not simply the lesser of two evils. The nature of "democratic" politics, in and of itself, requires compromise.

At the core of what is literally destroying American society is the breakdown of the nuclear family structure (system). Society begins and ends with family structure. Above all, God is the designer of the family, not the U.S. Supreme Court. God's will shall be done because "The earth is the Lord's, and the fullness thereof; the world, and they that dwell therein" (Psalms 24:1).

Without a doubt, the 2016 presidential election was a "socio-spiritual-revelation" about how nations fall from the grace of God, and tear down the spiritual and moral walls of society. The election of Donald J. Trump to the office of president exposed the underbelly of the racial divide that has spiritually plagued American society from the beginning. Of course, every American needs to pray that God will "Shew me thy ways, O Lord; teach me thy paths. Lead me in thy truth, and teach me: for thou art the God of my salvation; on thee do I wait all the day" (Psalm 25:4-5). But, more importantly, know full well that, "If my people, which are called by my name, shall humble themselves, and pray, and seek my face, and turn from their wicked ways; then will I hear from heaven, and will forgive their sin, and will heal their land" (2 Chronicles 7:14).

I thank my family for their loving support, especially my wife, Larnita; my son, Daryl Anthony; and my daughters, Kelly Leigh and Karen Rene'. Grateful appreciation and heartfelt thanks are extended to Charles W. Moore for our eternal friendship, Bible study time, and enlightening spiritual conversations. Thanks also goes to Pastor Robert E. Childress, Pastor Raymond L. Farley, Pastor John E. Cameron, Pastor Kelly Gene Reynolds, and Pastor Clifton Goodloe, Jr., for the spiritual based friendship over the years. I love and thank you all. To God be the glory and honor. Selah!

INTRODUCTION

How do we live is an eternal spiritual and moral question? More importantly, how do individuals learn to live beyond selfishness and in fellowship with God, and at the same time, learn to love and serve others in Jesus's name? These questions are from the two Great Commandments in Matthew 22:34-40. Relationships matter because individuals in relationships have spiritual and moral challenges. Challenges have both positive as well as negatives consequences. These are profound theological questions about life and creative living. Most individuals want to live to become elderly and die peacefully. On the other hand, some young individuals for strange and contestable reasons want to commit suicide because they cannot face the realities and challenges of living. However, God wants us to live eternally, love unconditionally, and serve one another faithfully in the name of Jesus.

American society is experiencing a "socio-spiritual" breakdown of moral order. Knowing how to raise money through the collection plate (Capitalistic Christianity), and teaching spiritual and moral order are vastly different. That is, knowing how to lead a nation to a higher level of spiritual and moral consciousness is another matter. Herein is the leadership problem both in Christendom as well as American secular society.

Following the spiritual tenets of the U.S. Constitution as an example in decision-making processes (words and deeds) the moral tenets therein are what make a nation great because, "Righteousness exalteth a nation, but sin is a reproach to any people" (Proverbs 14:34). America, we all know, what our leaders have said in the past concerning the moral state of affairs in American society, but, "When he speaketh fair, believe him not: for there are seven abominations in his heart. Whose hatred is covered by deceit, his wickedness shall be shewed before the whole congregation" (Proverbs 26:25-26). Forewarned is foretold. America chasing after the promises of the flesh, the promises of a rich man, and his money is like chasing after fool's gold. But, without a doubt, absolutely no knowledge of God's Word, "A little that a righteous man hath is better than the riches of many" (Psalm 37:16). Once again, American minorities are not worried about America becoming "great again" at their expense. America is already great, and when this presidential episode in America's history is all said and done, although many will suffer this too shall pass. We all know that the great equalizer in any society is death, because: "And as it is appointed unto men once to die, but after this the judgment" (Hebrews 9:27). We can fret not because, "God judgeth the righteous, and God is angry with the wicked every day" (Psalms 7:11). And, "Every word of God is pure: He is a shield unto them that put their trust in Him" (Proverbs 30:5).

The overwhelming majority of minorities are not overly concerned about the tenets of white privilege that are being espoused by "white nationalist Trump supporters." And, here's the Biblical reason why, "I have been young, and now am old; yet have I not seen the righteous forsaken, nor his seed begging bread" (Psalm 37: 25). All individuals should live in holiness and be spiritually happy. Leadership is not about putting on a fake reality show to an unfriendly increasingly secularized world, but it is about leading individuals to a higher level of spiritual and moral consciousness about the meaning of life. Leadership is not a show, but about showing that you can do the work spiritually, intellectually, and above all, create a team approach to the decision-making process. There is no "I" in team. The personal pronoun disease is a lethal human disease. In short, once a decision is made after discussing the pros and cons all must join in as one to ensure the best outcome.

The 2016 presidential election was about three factors: American culture, white nationalism, and anti-God consciousness with an ungodly emphasis on white privilege. Too many so-called Christian right evangelicals, white nationalists, and others with pent-up emotions concerning institutional racism enjoyed the divisive rhetoric. The racially and ethnically divisive rhetoric of President-elect Trump gave emotional ventilation to their minds.

Let's be perfectly clear about these historical social facts: (A) Native Americans have been in America from the beginning; (B) Blacks were a part of the initial development of American society brought here on slave-ships for free labor for white capitalism; and (C) Whites were not just to other Whites in Europe consequently bringing out the Great White Migration in order to institute white privilege in a foreign land.

Attempting to reclaim the past is doing the work of evil-minded men, the work of the devil. Simply put, the past belongs to the devil because the past is imperfect due to the free will that individuals have to make choices. God desires that individuals not repeat the sins of the past but follow the instructions of Jesus' two Great Commandments recorded in the Holy Bible. We all know that God works through men who will honor and obey His teachings as the life of Jesus Christ serves as an example. Therefore, God holds the future in His hands. Proverbs 23:7 states, "For as he thinketh in his heart, so is he". Even in an individual's feeble attempt to resurrect the past, we should all remember this spiritual fact, "God judgeth the righteous, and God is angry with the wicked every day" (Psalm 7:11). But, more importantly, God has the final say, the last word, and the final action in all things because, "Nevertheless the foundation of God standeth sure, having His seal, The Lord knoweth them that are His. And, let every one that nameth the name of Christ depart from iniquity" (2 Timothy 2: 19). Therefore, if an individual says that he or she is a Christian then you ought to be Christ-like in your love and service to others. If you are a Christian, you ought to show some sign by, "let this mind be in you, which was also in Christ Jesus" (Philippians 2:5).

In conclusion of the whole matter, in terms of why American society is in spiritual and moral turmoil and why our democratic institutions which have checks and balances on all Americans especially in our political and diplomatic institutions may not survive the "Trumpeter's" leadership style is vividly reflected in his lackadaisical approach to receiving daily presidential briefings. Someone needs to inform president-elect Trump that ignorance of the law is no excuse. Romans 1:18-20 states, "For the wrath of God is revealed from heaven against all ungodliness and unrighteousness of men, who hold the truth in unrighteousness; because that which may be known of God is manifest in them; for God hath shewed it unto them. For the invisible things of Him from the creation of the world are clearly seen, being understood by the things that are made, even his eternal power and Godhead; so that they are without excuse." This, my fellow Americans, is for real! The national news, especially the Presidential Press Corps need to give the "Good News Gospel" that is the truth, the whole truth, and nothing but the truth because "The Lord gave the word: great was the company of those that published it" (Psalm 68:11).

Finally, President-elect Donald J. Trump, your praising of Putin, a foreign dictator, an anti-American national security advocate has created an untenable condition for American social democracy. Russia cannot be trusted, the world knows it, and Donald J. Trump should know it as well. Apparently, when 500 billion dollars are involved in the equation it literally makes no difference. Based upon the intelligence reports of 17 different intelligence agencies, *The Washington Post* has linked Russia to cyber-meddling in America's presidential election process. Russia's sole purpose apparently was to tilt the presidential election in Donald Trump's favor. And, they succeeded with the help of Christian right evangelicals, working class whites, white nationalists who desire white privilege (something for nothing), and uneducated and educated white women. Many of the individuals who voted for Donald Trump are misguided in their naïve assumption that when minorities succeed it is at their economic expense. What a big white lie! Minorities are still the last hired and the first fired: Go tell that.

Republican opposition including President-elect Trump has given aid and comfort to the enemy of America's sovereignty and social democracy. Shame! Shame! Shame! On July 26, 1920, an editorial was written in the *Baltimore Evening Sun* by H. L. Mencken that emphatically declared, "As democracy is perfected, the office of the President represents, more and more closely, the inner soul of the people. On some great and glorious day, the plain folks of the land will reach their heart's desire at last, and the White House will be occupied by a downright fool and a complete narcissistic moron." This editorial comment is a prophetic spiritual word penned in 1920. Let's hope that it is not a Nostradamus prediction. But, just in case, Christian God-fearing Americans, let's pray that November 8th, 2016 was not that day. Selah!

1

THE DONALD TRUMP PHENOMENON: PAR FOR THE COURSE

Ecclesiastes 5:10 states, "He that loveth silver shall not be satisfied with silver; nor he that loveth abundance with increase: this is also vanity." To be sure, a fool will say in the heart of his mind that money answers all things (the vanity of life). Money changing is bad for soul salvation, because sometimes individuals attempt to buy and sell souls. "I know thy works, and tribulation, and poverty, (but thou art rich) and I know the blasphemy of them which say they are Jews, and are not, but are the synagogue of Satan" (Revelation 2:9).

Can American culture, especially the American political system, be liberated from the curse of money? I don't know. However, the jury is still out, but we all know how difficult it is for a rich man to go to heaven. Wealthy drug dealers are exalted in American culture above spiritually minded individuals, because of their wealth; even though they are selling death to the nation. Many young men are recruited into homosexuality lifestyles through drugs. And, by the way, many young women are recruited into prostitution seeking to sell something that is the gift of God - love. This is precisely why God hates prostitution.

Herein lies the Donald Trump phenomenon: Americans are

listening to Donald Trump simply because he has the platform of wealth and money, not because he has a good spiritual understanding concerning life. It seems as though some Americans are willing to vote against their own best interests and that of the nation for perceived white privilege. But, we all know, that beyond a shadow of doubt "Black lives matter." One of the wisest men recorded in Biblical history said it best, "I am black, but comely, o ye daughters of Jerusalem, as the tents of Kedar, as the curtains of Solomon. Look not upon me, because I am black, because the sun hath looked upon me" (The Song of Solomon 1:5-6).

The Bible says, "Answer a fool according to his folly, lest thou also be like unto him. Answer a fool according to his folly, lest he be wise in his own conceit. He that sendeth a message by the hand of a fool cutteth off the feet, and drinketh damage" (Proverbs 26: 4-6). But, more importantly, "When he speaketh fair, believe him not: for there are seven abominations in his heart" (Proverbs 26:25). The six deadly sins and the seventh is an abomination to God, "These six things doth the Lord hate; yea, seven are an abomination unto him: a proud look, a lying tongue, and hands that shed blood, a heart that deviseth wicked imaginations, feet that be swift in running to mischief, a false witness that speaketh lies, and he that soweth discord among the brethren" (Proverbs 6:16-19).

The love of money hinders the development of spiritual moral conscience, because individuals who have an abundance of money think they can buy anything and everything, including moral conscience as well as other individuals. Of course, anything money can buy is not necessarily good or bad, because money is simply a tool to advance a spiritual mindset be it good or bad. Listening to individuals simply because they are rich is always an unwise proposition because "And again I say unto you, it is easier for a camel to go through the eye of a needle, than for a rich man to enter into the Kingdom of God" (Matthew 19: 24).

The Bible is replete with spiritual examples of the potential curse of money upon an individual's life and lifestyle, because the deceitfulness of riches can choke off the Word of God, and an individual becomes spiritually unfruitful. Therefore, money is a tool that individuals should use as tools, not use as fools to enslave themselves to the vanity of this world. In case you have momentary lapses of knowledge (memory), earth is your natural habitat but trust me, not your home. Unfortunately, too many Americans use money as fools, which in turn, engender self enslavement. Sometimes even the good that rich individuals do with their wealth becomes bad, because of inappropriate spiritual motivations. Motive is the domain where sin resides, the devil's workshop. This is precisely why police agencies in seeking to solve crimes always first look for who has the motive plus the opportunity.

What is propelling the Trump phenomenon? What does the Trump phenomenon say about the philosophical tenets of the Republican Party?

Unfortunately, in the twenty-first century the answer to both questions is white privilege. That is, the dehumanizing vestiges of chattel slavery and institutional racism. The physical signs have been pulled down, but the heart of the mind of too many individuals have not changed. After a bloody Civil War, institutionalized Jim Crowism, institutionalized racism, a Civil Rights Act and a Voting Rights Act, the racial divide still remains as a color ordinated chasm. The American melting pot is simply a noble theory, not a living reality. Shame, shame, and more shame on the use-to-be party of Abraham Lincoln, who was an avid reader of the Holy Bible, because now the Republican Party is the "Dixiecrat Exclusionary Party" based upon white privilege.

All spiritually minded Americans should embrace this scripture, "And we know that all things work together for good to them that love God, to them who are called according to His purpose" (Romans 8:28). Selah!

2
MAKE AMERICA GREAT AGAIN!

Subliminal messaging has always been an integral part of the American political landscape and the 2016 presidential election was no exception. Everyone understands ungodly coded phrases. The phrase "Make America Great Again" is a troubling phrase that appeals to the dark side of American culture. When did America lose her greatness? The U.S. Constitution was written by great men with a lot of spiritual forethought from the Bible and many of them came to America to escape religious persecution. Thus, the U.S. Constitution was and still is one of the greatest nation-state governing documents that has ever been written, especially the Preamble to the U.S. Constitution. What a document. Sadly though, it is the framers who could not live up to the preamble, let alone the body of the Constitution.

Unfortunately, the Constitutional framers should have been more astute in researching the inspirational words of God in the Bible written by the Apostle Paul, "For I say, through the grace given unto me, to every man that is among you, not to think of himself more highly than he ought to think; but to think soberly, according as God hath dealt to every man the measure of faith" (Romans 12:3).

Young Americans, this is for your spiritual understanding and consideration, because most mature adults and Christian believers already know and understand that the phrase "Make America Great Again" is living the past without having the Godly understanding to embrace the future. In fact, the phrase is reflective of a spiritually dying nation that has a God problem, not a racial problem. Race is a social concept and construction, not a biological or a God concept.

The Bible clearly describes individuals who say one thing and then do another. Scripture says, "Woe unto you, scribes and Pharisees, hypocrites! for ye are like unto whited sepulchres, which indeed appear beautiful outward, but are within full of dead men's bones, and of all uncleanness. Even so ye also outwardly appear righteous unto men, but within ye are full of hypocrisy and iniquity" (Matthew 23:27-28). "All" means all. The Pharisees, Sadducees, and scribes were individuals who wore fine clothing, always wanted the best seats at the banquet table, used glowing language, and said long self-righteous prayers. But, after all is said and done, the Bible bestows upon them the status of hypocrites. And, the Bible is absolutely clear concerning false representation, and action always speaks louder than words, and inaction is sounding brass, and tinkling cymbals. "When he speaketh fair, believe him not: for there are seven abominations in his heart. Whose hatred is covered by deceit, his wickedness shall be shewed before the whole congregation" (Proverbs 26:25-26).

The framers of the Constitution were honorable men, and yet at the same time they were hypocrites, because some of them thought other men were not fully human. In the twenty-first century, we have untold numbers of double-minded individuals who desire privilege rather than equality of opportunity for all Americans. Saying one thing and doing another has serious consequences. However, the Word of God never returns void: "For as the rain cometh down, and the snow from heaven, and returneth not thither, but watereth the earth, and maketh it bring forth and bud, that it may give seed to the sower, and bread to the eater: so shall my word be that goeth forth out of my mouth: it shall not return unto me void, but it shall accomplish that which I please, and it shall prosper in the thing whereto I sent it" (Isaiah 56:10-11). Things can and will get better, but only through God. "Beloved, think it not strange concerning the fiery trial which is to try you, as though some strange thing happened unto you: but rejoice, inasmuch as ye are partakers of Christ's sufferings; that, when his glory shall be revealed, ye may be glad also with exceeding joy" (1 Peter 4:12-13).

Let's go further in our analysis of the statement "Make America Great Again!" What's not great in America? The answers are: healthcare, education, the tax code, wages and economic opportunities, urban ghettos, gender discrimination, the criminal justice system, and the environmental quality. Of course, for some citizens, America has never been great, because of the lack of opportunity.

In all of our varied and different perspectives about what is not great about America, America is still the greatest nation in the world. But, fortunately, we live in America, and what currently exists is not acceptable to the vast majority of Americans. Love it or leave it is not an option. Rather, change it or lose it can easily become a living reality.

Some readers will invariably ask the question: Who do you think you are questioning the motives of the framers of the U.S. Constitution? My answer is, no one is questioning the motives of the framers. However, the spiritual conscience of the framers of the Constitution is being questioned because the Bible says, "For I rejoice greatly, when the brethren came and testified of the truth that is in thee, even as thou walkest in the truth. I have no greater joy than to hear that my children walk in the truth" (3 John 1:3-4). Of course, the truth belongs to God, and the truth will make you free (John 8:32).

Being spiritually armed with the truth of God is essential in the last days of "Make America Great Again." Hebrews 2:3-4 states, "How shall we escape, if we neglect so great salvation: which at the first began to be spoken by the Lord, and was confirmed unto us by them that heard him; God also bearing them witness, both with great signs and wonders, and with divers miracles, and gifts of the Holy Ghost, according to his own will." America's fervent prayer should always be: "Sanctify them through thy truth: thy word is truth. As thou hast sent me into the world, even so have I also sent them into the world. And for their sakes I sanctify myself, that they also might be sanctified through the truth" (John 17: 17-19). Selah!

3

BEWARE OF INDIVIDUALS WITH ALL THE ANSWERS

A classic example of individuals with all the answers is Hitler in the past and Putin in the here and now. But, we all know that there has only been one Individual throughout human history with all the spiritual answers to every socio-economic-societal problem. That Individual is none other than Jesus. Societal injustice is indeed a spiritual problem because justice is spiritual (fairness). Individuals rejected Jesus and chose the thief and murderer Barabbas (Matthew 27:16-27). And we all know why. Some individuals want to play God even though we know that no individual can ever become God, since God cannot die, but all individuals die. Hebrews 9:27 says, "And as it is appointed unto men once to die, but after this the judgment." The time honored folklore statement that "death and taxes are certainties" has been debunked by the Trumpster. It seems as though he has not paid any federal income taxes in years. Trump, please pay your fair share of federal taxes so as to provide for domestic tranquility, promote the general welfare, provide for the national defense of America's borders, and redevelop America's crumbling infrastructure.

One of the most dangerous forces in the world is an individual who thinks he knows but knows not. This type of thinking is as dangerous as a category five hurricane. But, what is potentially more catastrophically dangerous are the followers of a so-called know-it-all personality who declares, "Trust me. I can fix it." The personal pronoun disease "I" is more often than not the "I" that is in the middle of SIN. As a nation-state, we embrace the Ronald Reagan doctrine: "Trust, but verify." Show us. Talk is cheap because six bankruptcies are economic indicators that you cannot handle your own personal finances. Why then should the American people trust you to handle public business or tax revenues especially since you do not pay your fair share of federal income taxes?

The moral will of the Preamble to the Constitution, as well as, the Articles of the Constitution should be done in all three branches of America's governmental system. It is not about a clown show or a puppet show but about American families. Let's not dismiss the social fact that economic life in American society has been on the decline. Workforce psyche preparation for twenty-first century job opportunities has been dismally lacking as well. Walk with me now through the reality of intellectually understanding how American society was transformed from an industrial society to a high-tech society. Computers and machines can do ninety percent of societal work resulting in manual labor becoming obsolete. It is extremely difficult for individuals with only a high school education to adapt to twenty-first century technological workforce needs. Cost effectiveness and the profit motive created the impetus for multinational corporations to take jobs overseas for cheap labor and create sweatshops on foreign soil. The federal government and trade agreements are not the problem. Corporate greed is the problem.

Many minority manual labor workers got caught up in the mix of this old adage: The last hired and the first fired. It is this process primarily that has escalated high minority unemployment.

Minorities did not cry, moan, and complain like the "Trumpster," "Make America Great Again." Many minorities simply are going back to school, seeking new skills and knowledge, and re-training opportunities to meet the workforce skill demands of the twenty-first century. Neither the Trumpster nor his followers can deny the "writing on the wall" (Habakkuk 2:1-3). The moving finger writes and moves on. Progress stops for no individual. Technology marches on and on and on. Therefore, individuals must learn to adapt to twenty-first century technological advances.

How do we spiritually, socially, politically, and economically change the political, greedy mindset madness landscape of American society? Individuals must stop doing the same ole same ole and expecting a different result. It was tried by Hitler and it failed. It is being tried by Putin, and it still will not be successful unless American leadership yields our democratic way of life to Putin. Be careful, American voters. You just might get what you want but absolutely not what you need. Change for the sake of change is not an answer, and sowing the "seeds of discord" is not an answer. The answer lies in the book of Proverbs written by one of the wisest man that ever lived because he asked God for wisdom that he might lead others into the path of righteousness. As is recorded, "Righteousness exalteth a nation: but sin is a reproach to any people" (Proverbs 14:34). America is truly in a time of great need. "Let us therefore come boldly unto the throne of grace, that we may obtain mercy, and find grace to help in time of need" (Hebrews 4:16).

Democracy is about maximizing the best interests of all citizens, not maximizing the insatiable greed of the corporate few. Republican Party officials who spiritually and intellectually know better ought to be ashamed of themselves for allowing the Trumpster to blow up the Republican Party. And thank God, a tape was leaked with Billy Bush and Donald Trump speaking negatively about women. This leaked tape allowed us to see who Trump really is: A man who utterly disrespects God's gift to men. Genesis 2:18 states, "And the Lord God said, It is not good that the man should be alone; I will make him an help meet for him." Without a doubt, men need women to help them meet their sacred obligations to God for there to be "peace on earth and good will toward men." Adam is the only man who did not have an earthly mother; however, all men need to spiritually understand that Adam did need a woman. Of course, Eve is the only woman who did not have an earthly father or mother. But, "Whoso findeth a wife findeth a good thing, and obtaineth favour of the Lord" (Proverbs 18:22).

All individuals are free to choose to do wrong because sin is a choice. God desires that individuals choose to love Him so that they might learn to love each other. Loving God is the answer, not glorifying Donald Trump because of perceived wealth. Obviously, the Trumpster only selfishly loves himself. All Americans should remember: "For as in Adam all die, even so in Christ shall all be made alive" (1 Corinthians 15:22). America, "Awake to righteousness, and sin not; for some have not the knowledge of God: I speak this to your shame" (1 Corinthians 15:34). Trust your God consciousness. Donald Trump is not America's Savior: Christ, the righteous one, is the Savior. Selah!

4

A SOCIO-RELIGIOUS VIEWPOINT ON POLITICAL GOVERNANCE

America is beyond the brink of a political governing disaster and on the edge of moral collapse. As a nation-state, we are caught in a political quagmire that no amount of money can resolve because of polluted minds, greed for money, thirst for power, and above all, a lack of moral will to do the right thing. Psalm 119:105 states, "Thy word is a lamp unto my feet, and a light unto my path". Make no mistake about it, this Scripture is real. And above all, a moral misunderstanding concerning the role and use of guns in a democratic society has become a monumental problem. Americans are armed to the teeth, and at the same time, scared to death. The real problem is an internal one. Ultimately, self is always the enemy. We looked for the enemy and found out that it is self. Let's face up to it, America. It is not a mental problem, but a spiritual and moral breakdown of the family unit.

One of the primary roles of institutional churches is spiritual and moral guidance. We are not training our children spiritually and morally to be productive citizens in our families, churches, or educational institutions. Taking prayer out of schools was a devilish idea and now the spirit of the devil is in schools. We are simply training children to exist in an immoral society. That is, we teach our children to question authority and to reject doing things decently and in order (1 Corinthians 14:33). If a child fails he/she should not blame society (individual responsibility), and society should not blame itself. Introspection and personal moral evaluation is always the key to a healthy and harmonious society. Choice is eternally the issue: right versus wrong.

The Democratic Party seeks to include all Americans in spite of ethnicity or immigrant status. However, the Democratic Party fails miserably to help all experience the American Dream. They cannot do it by themselves, so they compromise. Invariably, this approach to governance in many instances creates governmental dependency. The real downside of this approach to political governance is that many women feel they do not need a male head of the household. Society begins with family structure and males should head households. We are living in a society where government has become the head of the household, not a man; and taxpayers pay the family expenses. Of course, government is not God. God is the designer of family structure, not government.

On the other hand, the Republican Party seeks to empower the corporate structure (the few, the upper-class) at the expense of the many middle-class families. In the end, white privilege becomes the order of the day. This approach to political governance seeks to empower individuals to work for money, not spiritual and moral character development. Money is not God. God is God and they that worship Him must worship Him in Spirit and truth (John 4:24). Consequently, the corporate business structure of society is preferentially developed at the expense of spirituality and morality because it is all about money without compromise. The end result is that the moral fabric of society is diminished, and no healthy legislation is passed that benefits all. What both political parties are doing is counterproductive to a healthy democracy, and above all, against the will of God. Unfortunately, we have internalized a my way or the highway leadership mentality.

This political approach to democratic governance ends up becoming a no-win situation for America because God's way is the only way. Both political parties keep attempting to circumvent the spiritual principles included in the U.S. Constitution. Joshua 1:8 states, "This book of the law shall not depart out of thy mouth; but thou shalt meditate therein day and night, that thou mayest observe to do according to all that is written therein: for then thou shalt make thy way prosperous, and then thou shalt have good success." The Bible was our guide in the beginning and it ought to be our guide until Jesus returns. The problem is neither the Democratic Party nor the Republican Party. The real problem is a spiritual problem called sin, and greed has become the fuel. The real question is this: How does a democratic society build spiritual wealth from the inside out? Luke 12:15 states, "Take heed, and beware of covetousness: for a man's life consisteth not in the abundance of the things which he possesseth". There is a monumental spiritual and moral difference between riches and wealth. God owns it all, and every individual dies and leaves stuff behind. Therefore, "Praise ye the Lord. Blessed is the man that feareth the Lord, that delighteth greatly in His commandments. His seed shall be mighty upon the earth: the generation of the upright shall be blessed. Wealth and riches shall be in his house: and his righteousness endureth forever" (Psalm 112:1-3). Both riches and wealth are gifts of God (Ecclesiastes 5:19). The wealthy of the world need to understand God's five primary purposes for wealth because God does have a money test.

- God gives the power to obtain wealth (covenant relationship, Deuteronomy 8:18).
- God desires that we prosper and be in good health as our souls prosper (3 John 1:2).
- A righteous and godly society allows for every man to be able to provide for his household (1 Timothy 5:8).
- The purpose of wealth is to increase the fruits of your righteousness (2 Corinthians 9:10). It is not to build bigger barns to house your wealth and be merry.
- The purpose of wealth is self-actualization of God's purpose for an individual's life (Matthew 25:15, 31-46). In the end, "Inasmuch as ye did it not to one of the least of these, ye did it not to me." "For unto whomsoever much is given, of him shall be much required: and to whom men have committed much, of him they will ask the more" (Luke 12: 48).

Don't take my word. Ask the rich man who Jesus told to sell his riches and give the profits to the poor, and come and follow Him. We all know the rest of the story (Matthew 19:21). This is precisely why Jesus said, "It is easier for a camel to go through the eye of a needle, than for a rich man to enter into the kingdom of God" (Matthew 19: 24). America, let's be governed by the spiritual precepts of the Constitution because it was written for all, and good will should exist for all. In the spirit of Christmas, and honoring the birth of our Lord and Savior and the spiritual teachings of Jesus Christ, let freedom reign all over the world. Selah!

5

BLUE COLLAR MENTALITY VERSUS WHITE COLLAR MENTALITY

American society is structured upon a hierarchical, socio-economic class system: upper-class, middle-class, working-class, and the poor. Although all Americans are socialized into the universal values of God, family, and country, each social class has a distinct value orientation associated with it based upon economic status. Certain occupational positions in American society invariably require that individuals possess a particular mindset based upon social class value distinctions. The art of leadership effectiveness is to understand what makes a leader, a leader. Jesus was an effective leader because He was a positive example of His own teachings. To be sure, individuals can only cut the art of the deal with the devil, not God because God is not a dealmaker. God did not create blue collar, white collar, racial color distinctions or any other social class distinctions. "Jesus Christ the same yesterday, and today, and forever" (Past, Present, and Future; Hebrews 13:8). America, take heed, "The Lord gave the word: great was the company of those that published it" (Psalm 68:11).

All Christians know "When he speaketh fair, believe him not, for there are seven abominations in his heart" (Proverbs 26:25). This Scripture is referencing the seven deadly sins. By the way, any individual who would declare that he has nothing to apologize to God for has a dangerous paradigm mindset. Americans, watch him, because there are no perfect individuals on planet earth. "For as he thinketh in his heart so is he" (Proverbs 23:7). Without a doubt, only God is perfect. Someone once said, "You can fool all the people some of the time, and some of the people all the time, but you can't fool all the people all the time."

Christians know that alarm clocks do not wake up individuals. God wakes them up. Therefore, let's not take it for granted when we get up for only God wakes us up. Let us not forget that. If any individual believes that an alarm clock can wake up an individual, then take one to the graveyard and see how many individuals get up. We know that everyone who says "Lord, Lord" does not necessarily have God consciousness. Usually individuals who have this type of mindset are moving fast but are going nowhere.

The 2008 election of President Barack Obama and his subsequent reelection in 2012 revealed that the racial and ethnic divide in American society was beyond the symbolic dimension of mere physical skin color. Racism is a culturally institutionalized religious mindset cultivated in the misguided notion of white privilege. The White House is called the White House and painted white, not just for mere symbolism but for socio-economic reality conditions. Symbols motivate social behavior. God-fearing individuals know that an authoritarian personality should not be in the White House. Presently, we are in the midst of the 2016 presidential election, and a lion is roaring in the streets of American society seeking whom he can devour and creating artificial social class and ethnic and racial divisions based upon dangerous false notions of white male privilege. Prior to the 1964 Civil Rights Act and the 1965 Voting Rights Act, American society experienced the White Citizen Council; that is, white southern business men dressed in business attire possessing a Ku Klux Klan (KKK) mentality. Unfortunately, the more things change the more they remain the same. However, God is not fooled. Individuals reap what they sow because God is no respecter of artificially contrived social class distinctions. "Be not deceived: God is not mocked: for whatsoever a man soweth, that shall he also reap" (Galatians 6:5).

What is intellectually perplexing about the 2016 presidential election is that regional differences seem no longer to matter. There is no North, South, East, or West. The blue collar mentality and white collar mentality now transcend perceived social class value distinctions, as well as geographical regions. In New York state, the supposedly most cosmopolitan state in the United States where the melting pot city of the world community is located (New York City), now displays cultural confusion. In New York state, we are witnessing the coming together at the fork of the road of blue collar and white collar mentalities to protect white male privilege.

Whatever happened to "one nation under God, indivisible with liberty and justice for all"? It is apparent that white socio-spiritual frustration with lack of economic opportunities (jobs), Washington-style political governance gridlock, a vanity oriented national environment, and the permanent tanning of the nation toward minority-majority status is ripping off the false covering on white male privilege. Consequently, shifting white women into minority group status has proven to be a losing cultural proposition. In a socially fractured society of white male privilege, this is proving to be the undoing of white male arbitrariness. Because white women are treated similar to minority status individuals, they feel like a minority even though they play a major role in the voting population. Again, "For as he thinketh in his heart so is he" (Proverbs 23:7).

The Republican Party has totally abandoned the spiritually unifying principles of Abraham Lincoln. It is apparent to casual observers that the Republican Party needs a mental enema; that is, a spiritual and mental cleansing because inclusion is more productive than exclusion. When the Grand Old Party, in the greatest democratic nation in the world desires to place an authoritarian blue collar mentality in the White House something has drastically gone awry. Look out, America! National disaster is knocking on your door. It seems as though the Republican Party with its unholy alliance with the ole Southern Dixiecrat Party has been marching toward this disastrous end. False demagogue leaders are saying the same ole thing, over and over again. What they used to speak in coded language form now is spoken loud and boldly. They encourage other individuals to believe that it is alright to now say "whatever" in a straightforward offensive manner to whomever and whenever they feel the urge to offend others. They believe that they will be rewarded for offending whomever and whenever they so desire (I'll pay your court costs and fines). It has even become fashionable to use the phrase "whatever floats your boat." I leave you with the following verse, "Be not deceived: evil communications corrupt good manners" (1 Corinthians 15:33). Selah!

6
CAN WE ALL GET ALONG?

In 1992, on the third day of the Los Angeles riots, Rodney King's life was resurrected (divinely inspired), and he asked this now famous question: "People, I just want to say, can we all get along?" This writer is not attempting to compare the resurrection of Jesus with the lifestyle experiences of Rodney King because the resurrection of Jesus on the third day from the grave is a totally different spiritual story with a vastly different spiritual outcome. Given the turmoil in our governmental political system, economic system, and the level of mass gun violence in our society, this question seems most appropriate: "Why can't we all get along?" The answer seems to be blowing in the wind, and therefore, we need to change the direction of the wind. The social structure of American society has come unglued spiritually and morally, and above all, the socio-economic-political "movers and shakers" in the system are more dysfunctional than ever before, even though we are the greatest social democracy on planet earth.

It is God's amazing grace which allowed Rodney King, who lived on the cutting edge of dysfunctionality, to embrace the philosophical, spiritual, and moral tenet that all individuals ought to respect each other's human rights, since they come from God. Sadly, Rodney King received an undeserved brutal beating by individuals who were paid protectors of individual civil liberties (civil rights). The unwarranted suffering of Rodney King should serve as a reminder to all of us about the spiritual power of forgiveness present in each of us especially when we acknowledge that "there is one God, and one mediator between God and men, the man Christ Jesus; who gave himself a ransom for all, to be testified in due time" (1 Timothy 2:5). Rodney King, through undeserved suffering, realized that "greater is He that is in you, than he that is in the world" (1 John 4:4). "For all have sinned, and come short of the glory of God" (Romans 3:23). Without a doubt, "...being justified by faith, we have peace with God through our Lord Jesus Christ" (Romans 5:1). All Americans should give thanks to God for the redemptive suffering of Jesus the Righteous One.

The wise men followed the star of Bethlehem that led them to the manger. American Christians, what stars are you following? Is it the star of David? Or is it other astrological stars such as Pisces, Cancer, Leo, and so on? But, there is only one star: Jesus! Jesus! Jesus! Jesus is the Star of hope and salvation for the world. Every Christian should know Scriptures of inspiration because "Thou art worthy, O Lord, to receive glory and honor and power: for thou hast created all things, and for thy pleasure they are and were created" (Revelation 4:11).

In the sacred holiday season of giving and receiving, we should remember the birth, life, teachings, and suffering of Jesus the Righteous One. All Americans need to take one step backward, take a deep breath, slow their roll, and give thanks to God. This holy season is about Jesus because Jesus is the reason for the season. "For there is one God, and one mediator between God and men, the man Christ Jesus" (1 Timothy 2:5). During the season of spiritual love, joy, and peace all Christian Americans should "Humble yourselves therefore under the mighty hand of God, that He may exalt you in due time. Casting all your care upon Him; for He careth for you" (1 Peter 5:6-7). This can only be accomplished through personal faith because "...without faith it is impossible to please Him: for he that cometh to God must believe that He is, and that He is a rewarder of them that diligently seek Him" (Hebrews 11:6).

As Christian Americans, we should always and forever remember to do the following, "Thy word have I hid in mine heart, that I might not sin against thee. Blessed art thou, O Lord: teach me thy statutes" (Psalm 119:11-12). God requires that we should always forgive because God has forgiven us.

What Christmas brings is inculcated in the spiritual meaning of the manger. Every individual's soul wagon (body and spirit) must be hitched to a star, and that Star must lead to Bethlehem and eternal life because "This is life eternal, that they might know thee the only true God, and Jesus Christ, whom thou hast sent" (John 17:3).

The manger sociologically means common. Although Jesus was born in a stable, an uncommon setting, his parents Joseph and Mary were the salt of the earth. It makes no difference where you are born as long as you come to the spiritual understanding of the purpose God has for your life. Therefore, it is not about the place, but the spiritual purpose of your birth, because even before you were conceived in your mother's womb God knew you. "Before I formed thee in the belly I knew thee: and before you came forth out of the womb I sanctified thee" (Jeremiah 1:5).

"And we know that all things work for good to them that love God, to them who are called according to his purpose" (Romans 8:28). Spiritually, the manger represents God's eternal love, grace, forgiveness of sin, eternal life, and God's mercy in human form

(Jesus). God is "Spirit," and must be worshipped in spirit and truth because "God so loved the world, that He gave His only begotten Son, that whosoever believeth in Him should not perish, but have everlasting life" (John 3:16). The name Jesus represents humanity, and the title Christ represents divinity.

Church houses ought to be places of spiritual enlightenment (houses of prayer) and not Santa Claus-oriented secular church houses. The Christian church should be Peter's rock and Christ's church. This should be the name and the claim of our Lord and Savior Jesus Christ's church, and the very gates of hell shall not prevail against Peter's rock and Christ's church. "For God sent not his Son into the world to condemn the world; but that the world through him might be saved" (John 3:17). Christmas is a manger experience, not a department store experience. Within this Scriptural context the concept manger refers to individual choice. To be sure, an individual can choose to love and serve God by loving and serving others in the name of Jesus the Christ. To God be the glory. Selah!

7
CAN YOU BELIEVE THIS?

American social democracy is based upon a state's rights (slavery) protectionism philosophy rather than the principle of one person: one vote. This is precisely why the struggle for voting rights protection is an ongoing political struggle. For, without a doubt, the philosophical foundation of the Electoral College is based upon the principle of property rights (haves versus have nots). Can you believe that an individual overwhelmingly wins the popular vote but loses the election? Yes. It can happen, but only in America.

Individuals who think that they know but spiritually know not, are gladly rejoicing that Fidel Castro is dead. All Americans should be crying that the Trumpster was elected President of these United States of America, and the "free" world should be crying, as well. Without a doubt, the Trumpster has no earthly intentions of following the leadership institutional protocols that govern a social democracy. And, scripturally here's the reason why, "The rich man's wealth is his strong city, and as an high wall in his own conceit" (Proverbs 18:11). The naive followers of an "unrighteous rich man" shall reap the "whirlwind," because "before destruction the heart of man is haughty, and before honour is humility" (Proverbs 18:12). But, more importantly, "When your fear cometh as desolation, and your destruction cometh as a whirlwind: when distress and anguish cometh upon you. Then shall they call upon me, but I will not answer; they shall seek me early, but they shall not find me: For they that hated knowledge, and did not choose the fear of the Lord: They would none of my counsel: they despised all my reproof" (Proverbs 1:21-30). Thus saith the Lord.

Can you believe this: The majority of American voters did not vote for the Trumpster? Are the votes of the majority just like the prophetic voice of John the Baptist crying in the wilderness of spiritual ignorance? "The voice of one crying in the wilderness, prepare ye the way of the Lord, make His paths straight" (Matthew 3:3).

Can you believe this: That some men will drop to their knees for the Trumpster? Above all, that some women will accept feminine denigration in order to be a part of an immoral individual's presidential administration, especially after viewing the Billy Bush videotape? But, more importantly, that some other men who claim Christian right evangelical credentials will bow down to immorality? This is called getting in the weeds of unrighteousness. Words matter because once words are spoken they can never be taken back. Intellectual integrity says it all because integrity is about how individuals spiritually think and morally behave in given situations. Hence, there are only a few individuals of moral valor (e.g., Gideon's three hundred). Individuals of valor know how to love and serve others in the name of Jesus Christ.

Minorities in American society, especially Blacks, have existed and endured human denigration and undeserved suffering. Of course, minorities will survive the Donald J. Trump presidential administration because of faith in God, not government nor men. For after all, we know, that spiritually "the first shall be last and the last shall be first" (Heaven). For, in the end times, rest assured, "For unto us a child is born, unto us a son is given: and the government shall be upon His shoulder: and His name shall be called Wonderful, Counselor, the mighty God, the everlasting Father, the Prince of Peace" (Isaiah 9:6).

Can you believe that after almost four hundred years of institutionalized discrimination based upon skin color some individuals still harbor ill will toward others based upon skin color? To all Americans who hate other Americans based upon skin-color know full well that minorities love all regardless of skin color. But minorities will not accept the majority pissing on them and call it rain from Heaven. God hates racism, and He answers prayer. "For if the word spoken by angels was stedfast, and every transgression and disobedience received a just recompence of reward; how shall we escape, if we neglect so great salvation" (Hebrews 2: 2-3).

In general, minorities love all individuals and God hates discrimination based upon nationality and skin color. For example, Miriam and Aaron (Moses's sister and brother) criticized Moses because he married an Ethiopian woman, and God appeared before them in a cloud. "And the anger of the Lord was kindled against them; and he departed. And the cloud departed from the tabernacle; and, behold, Miriam became leprous, white as snow: and Aaron looked upon Miriam, and, behold she was leprous" (Numbers 12:9-10).

To be sure, the Trumpster is taking his power victory lap, consolidating his spiritually confused voting base. But, more importantly, the Trumpster is making innuendoes and threats toward the press and the loyal opposition: Get in line or else suffer the consequences. Without a doubt, if the press and the loyal opposition turn tail and succumb, and not spiritually fight for what is right for all Americans then they have created the demise of the institutional democratic institutions of a Great Society.

Listen, my fellow Americans, every day is the Lord's Day. And, in His day it is a time of reckoning, because God will make that which is crooked straight. "Wait on the Lord, and keep His way, and He shall exalt thee to inherit the land: when the wicked are cut off, thou shalt see it. I have seen the wicked in great power, and spreading himself like a green bay tree. Yet he passed away, and lo, he was not: yea, I sought him, but he could not be found. Mark the perfect man, and behold the upright: for the end of that man is peace. But the transgressors shall be destroyed together: the end of the wicked shall be cut off. But the salvation of the righteous is of the Lord: He is their strength in time of trouble. And the Lord shall help them, and deliver them: He shall deliver them from the wicked, and save them, because they trust in Him" (Psalms 37:34-40). Selah!

8

DOES AMERICAN SOCIETY DESERVE 2016 PRESIDENTIAL CONFUSION?

Presidential elections ought to be about federal governance issues, leadership qualities, and a spiritual, moral, intellectual and mental state of mind. Above all, as Abraham Lincoln stated, "A nation divided against itself cannot stand." Yet, all this trash-talking, speaking without facts, and telling outright lies should be morally off limits in any presidential primary. The presidency of the United States of America is serious moral business, because America should always be the moral conscience of the world community. The 2016 Republican Party primary process was about negativity, personality assassination, character assassination, gutter rat politics, and not about federal governance and governmental policies. The world has a Savior and Christians know how to create heaven on earth by following the two Great Commandments. When the will of God is done on earth as it is in heaven, we have heaven on earth (Matthew 6:9-13). Demagogues know absolutely nothing about the two Great Commandments, but an awful lot about the dark side of life: hooking, crooking, and using other people's money.

Hear this America, because we all know, "Righteousness exalteth a nation: but sin is a reproach to any people" (Proverbs 14:34). More importantly, "The wisdom of the prudent is to understand his (God's) way: but the folly of fools is deceit" (Proverbs 14:8). America, your moral compass is not being questioned, but what is being called into question is political support of white privilege oriented policies. America is the most sophisticated multi-cultural democratic nation-state in the world community. And, what happened in the Republican Party primary process is not normal, and those who believe that it was normal are indeed not normal.

"Make America Great Again" is not a policy because all Americans know that America is truly great. "Take My Word" and "Trust Me" are not policies. Most Americans are not willing to go down that rabbit trail: trusting without having verification. Donald Trump, give Americans a break because most Americans are not foolish. In fact, most Americans believe in the Ronald Reagan doctrine: "Trust, but verify." In short, "Answer not a fool according to his folly, lest thou also be like unto him" (Proverbs 26:4). But, without a doubt, "Answer a fool according to his folly, lest he be wise in his own conceit" (Proverbs 26:5).

In the 2016 presidential election immoral words are being spoken that provoke passion and emotions without spiritual substance, which in turn, can and do lead confused minds astray. In fact, if the Republican Party primary process had been about democratic statesmanship and federal governance policies, then one of the two sane-minded governors in the primary process would have been the Republican nominee. Presidential politics should never be about showmanship, an unbridled tongue, or animosity toward others. The press must always be the guardian of truth through the investigation of facts, and not allow hood-winking. But, fortunately, most Americans know hood-winking when it is presented to them; however, some Americans do not care because their love of white privilege is greater than their love of the truth and righteousness.

Unfortunately, the Republican Party primary process was about America's past, not the present moment or an inclusive future for all Americans regardless of skin color or ethnic origin. The past belongs to the devil, and of course, the past is imperfect. For after all, the past was not godly, but devilish; the future belongs to God. Hence, when some individuals seek to make the past moment the present moment it invariably creates spiritual and moral confusion in society. As Elvis Presley so eloquently stated some individuals will become "All Shook Up." Because, Godly Americans know that this too shall pass; therefore, "Be not deceived; God is not mocked: for whatsoever a man soweth, that he shall also reap. For he that soweth to the flesh shall of the flesh reap corruption: but he that soweth to the Spirit shall of the Spirit reap life everlasting" (Galatians 6:7-8). For after all, only, "Fools make a mock at sin: but among the righteous there is favor" (Proverbs 14:9).

Here's a little prudent advice to Americans who are following the Trump star for monetary gain reasons. Beware because Trump's monetary policy is based upon, "use other people's money." America, do you want to give Trump access to your tax dollars that is the U.S. Treasury?

Finally, this question must be asked of all Americans: Are you better off in 2016 than you were in 2008? Every American must answer in the affirmative, because American society is better off. Therefore, America as a nation-state simply needs to understand this scripture and the land will be healed, "If my people, which are called by my name, shall humble themselves, and pray, and seek my face, and turn from their wicked ways; then will I hear from heaven, and will forgive their sin, and will heal their land" (2 Chronicles 7:14). Amen! Amen! Amen!

9

FEAR CAN MAKE INDIVIDUALS SAY AND DO UNHOLY THINGS

Fear makes fools out of individuals if not bridled because "fools make a mock of sin: but among the righteous there is favor" (Proverbs 14:9). Therefore, "Trust in the Lord with all thine heart; and lean not unto thine own understanding. In all thy ways acknowledge Him, and He shall direct thy paths" (Proverbs 3:5-6). President Franklin D. Roosevelt said it best, "We have nothing to fear, but fear itself." But, more importantly, "The wisdom of the prudent is to understand his way: but the folly of fools is deceit" (Proverbs 14:8). The devil desires that individuals live in fear of man-made circumstances and social conditions in order to create confusion because confusion destroys. Yet, the fear of Almighty God is instruction in wisdom. First Corinthians 14:33 states, "For God is not the author of confusion, but of peace, as in all churches of the saints" (1 Corinthians 14:33). In this biblical context, church refers to the souls of individuals, not physical structures that are the embodiment of the visible but invisible church without walls. Of course, church begins with a moral conscience and is structured institutionally in family life.

As Christian Americans, we should not allow our unbridled fears to become the undoing of our civilized democratic processes because fear fuels the enemy's agenda. Herein lies the truth of the matter. The prophet Isaiah stated emphatically when faced with similar circumstances, "In righteousness shalt thou be established: thou shalt be far from oppression: for thou shalt not fear: and from terror: for it shall not come near thee" (Isaiah 54:14). Today, I personally know this scripture to be a powerful spiritual truth that can be inspirational to all because I was born in the dark days of racial oppression (institutional racism) that was prior to the 1964 Civil Rights Act and the 1965 Voting Rights Act. Therefore, all twenty-first century Christians can say the same thing first century Christians said, "The Lord is my helper, and I will not fear what man shall do unto me" (Hebrews 13:6). First century Christians were thrown in lion's dens, burned at stakes, crucified and experienced a lot of other unsavory ways of taking human life, but Christianity is still alive and standing for the righteousness of God because "Righteousness exalteth a nation, but sin is a reproach to any people" (Proverbs 14:34).

Why all the fear and rancor in American society? America has become a gun culture. American society has more guns than citizens. The question then becomes, do people feel secure with all of their guns? Or do they fear others because they have guns too? Let's be honest with ourselves: Maybe, we need to get guns checkmated legislatively. The First Amendment's right to life, liberty and the pursuit of happiness should be paramount, not guns. Of course, this is why it is the first amendment rather than the second amendment because "In God have I put my trust: I will not be afraid what man can do unto me" (Psalm 56:11). Without a doubt, a fearful fool can easily obtain a gun in a gun culture any day in the week and twice on Sunday. America, can you allow the Holy Spirit to give some sound spiritual advice? "Fear thou not: for I am with thee; yea, I will help thee, yea, I will uphold thee with the right hand of my righteousness" (Isaiah 41:10).

Allow me to take you to a spiritual higher ground with sound biblical doctrine, where the rubber meets the road. James 3:16-18 states, "For where envying and strife is, there is confusion and every evil work. But the wisdom that is from above is first pure, then peaceable, gentle, and easy to be intreated, full of mercy and good fruits, without partiality, and without hypocrisy. And the fruit of righteousness is sown in peace of them that make peace." It is hoped that America has not become so secular and humanistically oriented that sound biblical doctrine cannot take root in American consciousness.

Let's make no mistake about it, there have always been and will probably always be a want to be controllers of the world. These so-called leaders call for the misuse and abuse of others (the stranger concept). But, thank God all of them have failed. Think about Alexander the Great, Julius Caesar, Napoleon Bonaparte, Hitler, and Mussolini, to name a few.

There will always be many individuals who live in fear of all others who are not like themselves. There will be those who are willing to follow demagogues because of paranoia (fear). But, on the other hand, there will always be those of sound biblical doctrine and common sense who will above all else fear Almighty God. The Bible profoundly reminds all of us, especially Christians to be leery of double-minded leaders. Proverbs 26:25-26 states, "When he speaketh fair, believe him not: for there are seven abominations in his heart. Whose hatred is covered by deceit, his wickedness shall be shewed before the whole congregation." The Bible gives us the perfect way for God-fearing individuals to recognize these types of so-called leaders, and how to respond to them, "Answer a fool according to his folly, lest he be wise in his own conceit. He that sendeth a message by the hand of a fool, cutteth off the feet, and drinketh damage" (Proverbs 26:4-6).

It is not what some leaders are selling or what they want the American people to buy, but that other want-to-be-leaders will not vehemently reject the product or condemn divisive words. Silence is consent. Individuals can think anything they so desire privately, but ungodly words can divide a nation of immigrants especially since the only Native Americans are Native Indians. Of course, we all know, "For as he thinketh in his heart, so is he: eat and drink, saith he to thee; but his heart is not with thee" (Proverbs 23:7).

Fear can never bring peaceful consolation unless it is fear of God because as Psalm 30:5 states, "For his anger endureth but a moment; in his favor is life: weeping may endure for a night, but joy cometh in the morning." Jesus said, "Peace I leave with you, my peace I give unto you, not as the world giveth, give I unto you. Let not your heart be troubled, neither let it be afraid" (John 14:27).

Finally, one Chinese Proverb states, "If there is right in the soul, there will be beauty in the person; if there is beauty in the person, there will be harmony in the home; if there is harmony in the home, there will be order in the nation; if there is order in the nation, there will be peace in the world." Selah!

10

GODHEAD LEADERSHIP, PASTORAL LEADERSHIP, AND CONGREGATIONAL STEWARDSHIP

Godhead leadership (Father, Son, and the Holy Ghost) being Christ-like is what Christendom is all about. Thank God as Christians we do not have to ask the question that was asked by the scribe: "Which is the first commandment of all? And Jesus answered him, the first of all commandments is, hear, O Israel; the Lord our God is one Lord: and thou shalt love the Lord thy God with all thy heart, and with all thy soul, and with all thy mind, and with all thy strength: this is the first commandment. And the second is like, namely this, thou shalt love thy neighbor as thyself. There is none other commandment greater than these" (Mark 12:29-31). Without a doubt, this is the only way Christians can help build the Kingdom of God on earth as it is in heaven (Matthew 6:9-13). Kingdom building is about making God the center of one's life, loving and serving each other, in Jesus's name, and to God be the glory.

Jesus is the Good Shepherd, and pastoral leaders are called to be good under-shepherds, men of valor, moral character, and intellectual integrity. But, above all, men who know how to love, serve, protect and feed the flock with the unadulterated Word of God (2 Peter 3:18). Men of valor have been sanctified in the truth of God; therefore, Lord help pastoral leaders to grow in grace and knowledge of our Lord and Savior Jesus Christ and, "Sanctify them through thy truth: thy word is truth" (John 17:17). Therefore, if any man is determined to be Godly who can stop him, because, "What shall we say to these things? If God be for us, who can be against us?" (Romans 8:31). I personally know a pastoral leader who was determined to be godly, Dr. William Phillip Diggs of Florence, South Carolina. Dr. Diggs taught me introductory sociology for two semesters at Friendship College and was the inspirational spirit of the Friendship Nine (Rock Hill, South Carolina Civil Rights Leaders, 1961). The Friendship Nine was nine college students during the Civil Rights Movement who chose to remain in jail rather than post bail after a sit-in demonstration at McCrory's restaurant in Rock Hill, South Carolina.

Dr. Diggs, through his college experiences in Atlanta, Georgia, at Morehouse College and Atlanta University, met and married the effervescent, delightful, charming, and congenial Clotilda Daniels, a powerful woman of God. Without a doubt, Godly men know, especially pastoral leaders that, "Whoso findeth a wife findeth a good thing, and obtaineth favour of the Lord" (Proverbs 18: 22). To this matrimonial union was born two godly children, William Phillip Jr. and Mary Lynne.

Recently, my wife and I visited Dr. Diggs and his family in Florence, South Carolina, and discovered that God plus William Phillip Diggs equals success in Jesus' name, and the glory belongs to God. Here's what my wife and I witnessed: A congregation with approximately 800 individuals on the church rolls, no congregational confusion, and approximately 300 in attendance each Sunday: Gideon's three hundred (the Lord's three hundred). We all know, especially Christians and pastoral leaders, "For God is not the author of confusion, but of peace, as in all churches of the saints" (1 Corinthians 14:33).

Under the pastoral leadership of Dr. Diggs, Trinity Baptist Church owns an entire city block, no financial debts, cash assets that exceeds several million dollars for benevolence and mission work, and a church-owned credit union with millions of dollars that was established in 1978 for church members and their relatives, which provides them with low interest rate loans on home mortgages and cars. Now that is a blessing!

Dr. Diggs recently retired after fifty years of under-shepherding Trinity Baptist Church, and the power of the following scripture was the cornerstone principle of his leadership, "Verily, verily I say unto to you. He that heareth my word, and believeth on Him that sent me, hath everlasting life, and shall not come into condemnation: but is passed from death unto life" (John 5:24). Pastoral leaders, a word to the wise is sufficient: Let the church be the church and God will be glorified, the name Jesus will be lifted-up above all names, and the Christian church will be the light of the world. "For there is one God, and one mediator between God and men, the man Christ Jesus; who gave himself a ransom for all, to be testified in due time" (1 Timothy 2:5-6).

It was spiritually refreshing to see at least one pastoral leader keeping faith with the historic tradition of church and community working together to improve socio-economic conditions in a local community. The Black community needs more pastoral leaders like Dr. Diggs who make a real difference in the lives of families, because we all know that Christianity is a central feature of the

Black experience in American society. In the past, the Black church served as the mainstay and the center of all community development, especially the Baptist church. Unfortunately, in the twenty-first century this is seemingly no longer the case. The question is what happened? When did the socio-economic paradigm change? Did Blacks become too obsessed with vanity, spiritually confused concerning the things of this world, and immorally intoxicated with the pleasure principle (drinking the world's Kool-Aid)? But, more importantly, Blacks abandoned the spiritual moral order of God, and forgot to "be sober, be vigilant; because your adversary the devil, as a roaring lion, walketh about, seeking whom he may devour: whom resist stedfast in the faith, knowing that the same afflictions are accomplished in your brethren that are in the world" (1 Peter 5:8-9).

Simply put, godly pastoral leadership breed's godly followership, because a godly under-shepherd knows how to shepherd God's people in the midst of suffering (redemptive suffering), trials, and tribulations. "Trust in the Lord with all thine heart; and lean not unto thine own understanding. In all thy ways acknowledge him, and he shall direct thy paths" (Proverbs 3:5-6). Therefore, in truth render under Caesar that which belongs to Caesar, and unto God that which belongs to God. Just a reminder to all: you belong to God. "What? Know ye not that your body is the temple of the Holy Ghost which is in you, which ye have of God, and ye are not your own? For ye are bought with a price: therefore glorify God in your body, and in your spirit, which are God's" (1 Corinthians 6:19-20). Selah!

11
GUTTER RAT POLITICS

The 2016 Presidential Republican Party primary process was hijacked by a gutter rat political mentality. Republicans, was it worth it? America appears to be on the brink of a national disaster because scientific knowledge, logical reasoning, political and language civility, and simply being a gentleman-like statesman was not a part of the political equation in the Republican Party primary process. The presidency of the United States of America is a serious national and international proposition. It is not a reality show. The presidency of the United States is about families, international business relationships (trade agreements), and peace and stability in the world community. Lest we forget, society begins and ends in family structure. The failure of the Republican Party primary process is proving to be disastrous for the spiritual well-being of the nation that we all love because a healthy two-party political system continues to be in the best interest of all Americans, as well as, the world community. A one-party political system is not healthy politics but a recipe for political governance chaos.

Seemingly, the leadership-style of former Governor George Wallace is alive and doing very well in American political life: "segregation today, segregation tomorrow, and segregation forever.". Yet, on the other hand, there were several experienced governors running on the Republican ticket who were well-trained, well-bred governmental civic leaders, and these highly qualified individuals were trash-talked out of the Republican

Party primary process. Why? Sadly, based upon their intellectual integrity and moral character they chose to not attend the Republican National Convention in Cleveland, Ohio. Indeed, some serious political soul-searching must take place in the philosophical and ideological psyche of the Republican Party. To what end does the Republican Party exist? Earthly leaders are made (groomed and trained), not born. Only one individual was born as a godly, heavenly Leader, and His name is Jesus, the righteous One. And, all earthly individuals sin and come short of the glory of God. King David said it best, "Wash me thoroughly from mine iniquity, and cleanse me from my sin. For I acknowledge my transgressions: and my sin is ever before me" (Psalm 51:2-3). Presidential leadership is not about the "art of a business deal", but spiritual conscience, intellectual integrity, moral character, and above all, an individual's desire to love and serve others. Moreover, presidential leadership is about setting a positive example, the fostering of national and societal priorities, and bridging the socio-religious divide in society between the college-educated and the non-college-educated because information technology has transformed American society. Democracy is about inclusion, not exclusion or privileges for one social group over another social group. This is precisely why social democracy requires an educated citizenry and why the founders instituted a mass universal educational system.

Without a doubt, the Republican Party of the twenty-first century has fueled a socio-religious cultural divide in American society. As a result, at the center of America's societal division is the color-line divide (racial divide). And, above all, at the heart of what is fueling this societal divide is the so-called religious right. Pure religion undefiled before God unites, not divide. "If any man among you seem to be religious, and bridleth not his tongue, but deceiveth his own heart, this man's religion is in vain. Pure religion and undefiled before God and the father is this, To visit the fatherless and widows in their affliction, and to keep himself unspotted from the world" (James 1:26-27). Genuine faith does not favor the rich because "Verily I say unto you. That a rich man shall hardly enter into the Kingdom of Heaven. And again I say unto you, it is easier for a camel to go through the eye of a needle, than for a rich man to enter into the Kingdom of God" (Matthew 19:23-24).

The election of President Barack Obama in 2008 triggered an unhealthy societal and political reaction on the part of the leadership of the Republican Party. When statements like the following were made: "our objective is to make him a one term President" and "we are not going to allow him to get any legislation passed" it reflected the epitome of one being malnourished in the brain. And, to top it off the birther movement was an absolute insult to the intelligence of all Americans. Therefore, it helped to fuel the socio-religious cultural divide in American society. As a result, Americans have become more distrustful of each other. Of course, the birther movement was designed to delegitimize the Obama presidency by declaring that he was not a legitimate American citizen. To be sure, this was an ungodly disguise for institutional racism.

Here's the long and short of what the 2016 Presidential election is all about: "Make America White Privilege Oriented Again". It cannot happen simply because too many white male workers are not technological skilled or college educated, but desire top shelf wages in order to provide their families with suburban homes, luxurious cars, and their children with college educations (the typical American dream). Working class white males want a middle class lifestyle without acquiring a college education. In fact, white working class males desire a middle-class lifestyle at the expense of minorities because they refuse to re-educate themselves for available twenty-first century technical jobs. White working class males, stop crying, mourning, groaning because the greed of multinational corporations shipped your jobs overseas, not the federal government. Therefore, re-educate and retrain yourselves for the technological jobs available in the twenty-first century. Above all, stop believing the ungodly spiritual nonsense of the religious right. God made us all, regardless of skin color, for His glory. If we truly believe that the "Earth is the Lord's and the fullness thereof" (Psalm 24:1) then all Americans should understand that even with our trials and tribulations America is a great nation. "We are troubled on every side, yet not distressed; we are perplexed, but not in despair; persecuted, but not forsaken; cast down, but not destroyed" (2 Corinthians 4:8-9). Therefore, as Americans, we must be spiritually sober, morally vigilant, and not allow the fox to get in the hen house. "Be sober, be vigilant; because your adversary the devil, as a roaring lion, walketh about, seeking whom he may devour: whom resist steadfast in the faith, knowing that the same afflictions are accomplished in your brethren that are in the world" (1 Peter 5:8-9). Selah!

12

IF YOU TALK THE TALK YOU SHOULD WALK THE WALK

We live in an age of decadent moral confusion, and God-fearing Christians should never give place to our ever present adversary, the devil. Unfortunately, it seems as though the adversary knows more Scripture than Christians (churchgoers). The devil tempted Jesus with material things and intangibles (Matthew 4:1-11). Is it because churchgoers cannot read? Is it because churchgoers are lazy and do not want to read? Or is it because churchgoers want to be told what to do, what to believe, and not know for themselves what the word of God truly says? This is why 3 John 1:2-3 says: "Beloved, I wish above all things that thou mayest prosper and be in good health, even as thy soul prospereth. For I rejoiced greatly, when the brethren came and testified of the truth that is in thee, even as thou walkest in the truth."

We have too many so-called Christian believers in America who are talking the talk, but not willing to walk the walk. As a Christian faith-walker, I personally would rather see a sermon than to hear a sermon. But, what a joy divine it would be to experience both together as word and action in the truth of God. The ultimate role of the church is to help make life real in the Living Word in the communities which they reside. This is the reason why the church was established upon Peter's faith in Jesus without ever building a physical structure (church house). "For this man was counted worthy of more glory than Moses, inasmuch as he who hath builded the house hath more honour than the house. For every house is builded by some man, but he that built all things is God" (Hebrews 3:3-4).

With all of the confusion in universal humanity (families, churches, educational institutions, and nation-states) beware my fellow Americans: "For if the word spoken by angels was stedfast, and every transgression and disobedience received a just recompence of reward; how shall we escape, if we neglect so great salvation..." (Hebrews 2:2-3). And, to be sure, Christians should not receive the grace of God in vain because "For he saith, I have heard thee in a time accepted, and in the day of salvation have I succoured thee: behold, now is the accepted time; behold, now is the day of salvation" (2 Corinthians 6:2). Individuals should never become so intelligent and puffed-up until they out-smart themselves (blow-up), because "Blessed are they that hear the word of God, and keep it" (Luke 11: 28). This is what all Christians should practice: "Thy word have I hid in mine heart, that I might not sin against thee" (Psalm 119:11). Therefore, this writer knows beyond a shadow of a doubt that "God is not the author of confusion, but of peace, as in all churches of the saints" (1 Corinthians 14:33). If you are not a saint, you should be a saint in God. Get right, do right and live right in the word of God.

All of us must come to a clear spiritual understanding of the importance of Jesus Christ's life whether Jew or Gentile, Protestant or Catholic, black or white or male or female, because it is written: "Verily, verily, I say unto you, he that heareth my word, and believeth on him that sent me, hath everlasting life, and shall not come into condemnation: but is passed from death unto life" (John 5:24). The essence of Jesus's spiritual importance is recorded in 1 Peter 2:24-25, "Who his own self bare our sins in his own body on the tree, that we, being dead to sins, should live unto righteousness: by whose stripes ye were healed. For ye were as sheep going astray; but are now returned unto the shepherd and Bishop of your souls."

Again, we live in difficult morally decadent times. Indeed, American society is in spiritual and moral free fall decline. But, regardless of the times in the bye and bye, 2 Corinthians 5:10 says, "For we must all appear before the judgment of Christ, that every one may receive the things done in his body, according to that he hath done, whether it be good or bad."

America needs to become the nation that God has called her to be, and embrace spiritually what the founding fathers envisioned. Americans talk that talk concerning justice and mercy, proclaiming "Give me your tired, your poor, your huddled masses yearning to be free, The wretched refuse of your teeming shore. Send these, the homeless, tempest-tossed to me, I lift my lamp beside the golden door!" These sacred words are inscribed on the Statue of Liberty. Do we really desire to live up to this sacred declaration? For if an individual fears losing his life, he has already lost it. Creative living requires courage. Jesus said it best in John 14:27-28, "Peace I leave with you, my peace I give unto you: not as the world gives, give I unto you. Let not your heart be troubled, neither let it be afraid." Some Americans, especially some Bible-belt Christians need a strong dose of spiritual backbone, and I pray to God that this Scriptural reference provides the antidote to their fears. "Let the words of my mouth, and the meditation of my heart, be acceptable in thy sight, O Lord, my strength, and my redeemer" (Psalms 19: 14). Is the declaration "Give me your tired and poor" simply empty words? Or is it sounding brass and tinkling cymbals?

Let every American come in humility before God's throne of grace, loving-kindness, and mercy that we might find the spiritual strength to help in time of great need, because "The fear of the Lord is the instruction of wisdom, and before honour is humility" (Proverbs 15:33). More importantly, "Let us therefore come boldly unto the throne of grace, that we may obtain mercy, and find grace to help in time of need" (Hebrews 4:16). Christian Americans, this scripture describes who we are! If you talk the talk, you should be able to walk the Christian walk as a faith-walker.

In conclusion of the whole matter, "But be ye doers of the word, and not hearers only, deceiving your own selves. For if any be a hearer of the word, and not a doer, he is like unto a man beholding his natural face in a glass: For he beholdeth himself, and goeth his way, and straightway forgetteth what manner of man he was. But whoso looketh into the perfect law of liberty, and continueth therein, he being not a forgetful hearer, but a doer of the work, this man shall be blessed in his deed" (James 1:22-25). Selah!

13

Is Life Too Cheap?

Am I my brother's keeper? The answer is a resounding yes. Knowing this socio-spiritual fact of life, why are so many blacks killing each other all the time? What is it that makes a man a man? Is it the ability to kill? Therefore, is taking another man's life or any human being's life a manly act? Or is it an act of cowardice?

We know that who the devil seeks to destroy, he first must make angry (Ephesians 4:26-27). Without a doubt, if a man cannot control his temper he is not a man, but a lower form of animal life. Black on black killing is the clearest spiritual example of the breakdown of the family structure, the spiritual failure of black churches, the mis-education of blacks in educational institutions, and a complete sense of community lawlessness. Couple these socio-spiritual dysfunctions with the attitudinal disposition of police constabularies that do not give a damn about your community. And what you have is a hell on earth and not the Kingdom of God on earth, as it is in heaven, and as is prayed for in the Lord's Prayer. Without a doubt, most individuals are living in hell and have become comfortable in spiritual confusion and social dysfunction.

The system has "singled-out" blacks for dehumanization and persecution, and seemingly our pastoral leaders, political leaders, and educational administrators have no answers for the horrible mess we find ourselves in nor do they provide solutions for why the mess exists! Maybe they do not have a clue concerning what to do. To be sure, far too many of our young people are destroying each other through personal and gang related violence. Behold, black America (all Americans): "The earth mourneth and fadeth away, the world languisheth and fadeth away, and the haughty people of the earth do languish. The earth also is defiled under the inhabitants thereof; because they have transgressed the laws, changed the ordinance, broken the everlasting covenant" (Isaiah 24:4-5). Black on black crime is an abomination, and this scripture helps all of us to understand the spiritual implications of man's inhumanity to man: "Before destruction the heart of man is haughty, and before honor is humility" (Proverbs 18:12).We need to learn how to use humility to lift one another up, rather than violence (destruction) to destroy each other. Let's call this exactly what it is, that is, call a spade a spade, a diamond a diamond, and a heart a heart.

Initially, there were 613 Old Testament laws, God reduced the 613 Old Testament laws to the Ten Commandments given to Moses, and Jesus clarified the Ten Commandments by referencing the Two Great Commandments (Matthew 6:36-40). The desire of the "human spirit" in the Black community ought to be to "spiritually" embrace the Ten Commandments, and especially these two: "Thou shalt not kill" (Number 6 of the 10) and, "Thou shalt not steal" (Number 8 of the 10). The ungodly level of killing in the black community is destroying the spiritual and moral fabric of the community, but more importantly, senseless killings are shutting off the Kingdom of Heaven.

The black community is going to hell in a handbasket by embracing man-made (worldly) laws that we know are against the will of God (God's Law), and seemingly this is the root cause of why so many of our children are spiritually confused. "For God is not the author of confusion, but of peace, as in all churches of the saints" (1 Corinthians 14:33). Black people of America, we should have learned this lesson through our spiritual journey in these United States of America from 1619 (slavery), 1863 (Emancipation Proclamation), 1954 (Brown-vs.-Board of Education), 1964 (Civil Rights Act), 1965 (Voting Rights Act), 2008 (the Election of President Obama), and 2012 (Reelection of President Obama). The spiritual lesson is simply this: "Righteousness exalteth a nation: but sin is a reproach to any people" (Proverbs 14:34).

Too many of our black youth are growing up substituting street-gangs (a posse mentality) as a surrogate family structure, seeking to resolve value and personality conflicts violently, rather than non-violently. Violence and more violence is not the answer. Loving things (an external value system) and using people is not the answer. The devil deals in things and death, and his desire is to get individuals to deal in things and death. For example, the devil tempted Jesus by encouraging him to deal in things. "If thou be the Son of God, command that these stones be made bread" (Matthew 4:3-4). "Then the devil taketh him up into the holy city, and setteth him on a pinnacle of the temple, and saith unto him, If thou be the Son of God, cast thou self down: ...Jesus said unto him, it is written again. Thou shalt not tempt the Lord thy God" (Matthew 4:5-7). "Again, the devil taketh him up into an exceeding high mountain, and sheweth him all the kingdoms of the world, and the glory of them, and saith unto him, All these things will I give thee, if thou wilt fall down and worship me. Then saith Jesus unto him, Get thee hence, Satan: for it is written, Thou shalt worship the Lord thy God, and him only shalt thou serve" (Matthew 4:8-10). The devil is a liar and the truth is not in him, and he cannot give what does not belong to him. "And Moses said unto him, As soon as I am gone out of the city, I will spread abroad my hands unto the Lord; and the thunder shall cease, neither shall there be any more hail; that thou mayest know that the earth is the Lord's" (Exodus 9:29). Just in case your carnal mind is like the mind of Pharaoh, Psalms 24:1 is spiritual food for thought: "The earth is the Lord's, and the fullness thereof; the world, and they that dwell therein" (Psalms 24:1).

Christian churches must find creative spiritual ways to strengthen family life in the black community, as well as, in American society in general, and at the same time, foster a more spiritual value orientation in thought patterns: "For to be carnally minded is death; but to be spiritually minded is life and peace. Because the carnal mind is enmity against God: for it is not subject to the law of God, neither indeed can be. So then they that are in the flesh cannot please God" (Romans 8:6-8).

When will black lives matter to blacks? Indeed, it is the Holy Spirit that frees us from sin; especially the sin of killing that is in violation of the sixth commandment: "Thou shalt not kill". A word to the spiritually wise is sufficient: "Don't take what you cannot give." God says: "Before I formed thee in the belly I knew thee:" (Jeremiah 1:5). Above all, "Lo, children are an heritage of the Lord: and the fruit of the womb is his reward" (Psalms 127:3). Selah!

14
KNOWLEDGE AND IQ IN A
SOCIAL DEMOCRACY

Say it ain't so. The foolishness taking place during the 2016 Presidential election can truly destroy a democratic nation-state. America, you know it, I know it, and world sees it. Yet, there are too many Americans simply seeking a change for the sake of change. And, of course, the change some Americans desire will bring about the collapse of American society: foretold is forewarned. The 2016 presidential election is an IQ test, but above all, a moral conscience test on what is the true spiritual meaning of American social democracy. The world is watching and waiting to see the results of the 2016 presidential election. The question is: what's next, America? Do we want a country of foolishness and chaos or a country that lives out the true meaning of the American dream? Without a doubt, "The house of the wicked shall be overthrown: but the tabernacle of the upright shall flourish" (Proverbs 14:11). Be vigilant, America, God is spiritually watching! The 2016 presidential election is a spiritual conscience referendum on whether or not Americans can love and serve God by loving and serving each other. Because, godly Americans know, that children of God understand: "Seek ye first the kingdom of God, and his righteousness; and all these things shall be added unto you" (Matthew 6:33).

The 2016 presidential election is a moral conscience test for American society, as well as the world community. And, if

Americans make the wrong decision the whole world is in mucho grande trouble. Therefore, the questions are:

- Can we all become loyal Americans?
- Can we all live out the true meaning of the Preamble to the U. S. Constitution?
- Can all Americans live out the true meaning of the U.S. Constitution itself?

The survival stakes are indeed very high, because the survival of future generations of Americans weighs in the balance. Therefore, believe God's message to America that states, "Behold I stand at the door and knock: if any man hear my voice, and open the door, I will come into him, and will sup with him, and he with me" (Revelation 3:20).

God has a spiritual IQ test message for twenty-first century Christian churches. The Messenger (Jesus Christ the Righteous One) has not changed. Therefore, do not change the message for the sake of privilege for the few: "Jesus Christ the same yesterday, and today, and forever" (Hebrews 13:8). God also has a spiritual message for the Christian right evangelical movement, because your involvement in the political process has not spiritually improved the IQ of the body politics. My spiritual Christian evangelical brethren heed this spiritual and political message: "There is no wisdom nor understanding nor counsel against the Lord" (Proverbs 21:30). Hopefully, this Scripture will prick your moral conscience, by sanctifying you in the truth of God that equal is equal, not equal is more or less equal, because we all know that silence is consent, not golden.

In 1992, Rodney King received an undeserved brutal beating by individuals who were paid protectors of civil liberties and civil rights. This brutal police beating ignited the Los Angeles riots. On the third day of the riots, Rodney King asked this question: "Can we all get along?" The 2016 presidential election is asking America that same question in a more profound spiritual, socio, political context: "Can America lead the free world by morally correct, positive examples and not by selling wolf tickets, and above all, not by the barrel of guns?" To be sure, we all know that America is not going to mess with fools with nuclear weaponry. That is potentially provoking a nuclear war. This is why one person talking about other people acquiring nuclear weapons is completely foolishness to the nth degree. Supporting and encouraging nuclear proliferation is an insane proposition.

One presidential candidate has viciously called the other "crooked", while at the same time, displaying to the world community, by words and actions, that he is both a crook and an emotionally unhinged individual. Can America governmentally manage both "crook" and "krazy", at the same time, without fostering national disaster? America, the Wise Men followed the Star of Bethlehem that led them to the manger, and we all know that the manger teaches us a profound spiritual lesson about life. America, what stars are you following? Is it the Star of Bethlehem? Or is it the evil star of Trump, that is, fool's gold? Because, without a doubt, the Trump star represents utter moral confusion, political confusion, as well as, international monetary confusion. Those individuals that think they will receive a dollar will be hollering. And, of course, we all know: "God is not the author of confusion, but peace, as in all churches of the saints" (1 Corinthians 14:33). In fact, Trump's antics, his unbalanced behavior, and hateful statements against non-whites has exposed the thin veiling that America thought hid her historical past of institutional racism, sexism, and religious bigotry. America, prepare for the eternal bonfire, because the fire is on its way, and both the righteous and the unrighteous shall be consumed.

America, our social history should inform us, and our religious understanding should guide our social interaction with each other, because we all know: "What then shall we say to these things? If God be for us, who can be against us?" (Romans 8:31). Only Americans (your vote) can save America from itself, because the 2016 presidential election is truly an IQ test. Selah!

15
THE MISSING MORAL LINKS

Life is about priorities. A priority is a value ordering of one's life. Values dictate institutional structures as well as family lifestyles. Learning how to order one's personal and family lifestyle in terms of intellectually knowing and spiritually understanding where to place one's ultimate trust is of primary importance. Vanity is spiritually dangerous because vanity creates debt, and debt is a form of slavery. This is precisely why the Bible declares, "Owe no man anything, but to love one another: for he that loveth another hath fulfilled the law" (Romans 13:8). Love fulfills God's requirements. Drinking the vanity of the world and not thinking is a bad combination, because life is ultimately about making mistakes. Every individual makes mistakes, but it is not the mistakes that individuals make; it is the inability of individuals to change, that is, to learn to live in spite of their mistakes. Someone once said, "Doing the same thing over and over is the classic definition of insanity." Real change comes from having societal knowledge, spiritual knowledge, and a personal relationship with God. 1 John 1:6-7 says, "If we say that we have fellowship with him, and walk in darkness, we lie, and do not the truth: but if we walk in the light, as he is in the light, we have fellowship one with another, and the blood of Jesus Christ his Son cleanseth us from all sin." Let's be clear about this particular Scripture, because this Scripture does not mean entitlement to salvation and being born again. It is only the first step in the process of salvation. For every individual must experience sanctification: "Sanctify them through thy truth: thy word is truth.

As thou hast sent me into the world, even so have I also sent them into the world. And for their sakes I sanctify myself, that they also might be sanctified through the truth" (John 17:17-19). Every individual must understand the process of receiving spiritual salvation, and therefore, understand this Scripture, because all of us sin either through omission or commission. Second Peter 3:18 says, "But grow in grace, and in the knowledge of our Lord and Savior Jesus Christ. To him be glory both now and forever. Amen." Therefore, every individual must acknowledge this Scriptural reference step: "Jesus answered, Verily, verily, I say unto thee, Except a man be born of water and of the Spirit, he cannot enter into the kingdom of God." (John 3:5). As the saying goes, "Get off the premises and get on the promise."

Above all, spiritually understanding what are the most important things about living a spiritually meaningful, fulfilling life is the key to having a successful life rather than merely having material success in life. This is why Jesus always spiritually confronted individuals with this question: Where do you place your ultimate trust, that is, whom do you love the most: the Creator or the creation? Counting the spiritual cost is a very important element in living a spiritually meaningful life. This is why Jesus always urged individuals to count the cost, because: "Take heed, and beware of covetousness: for a man's life consisteth not in the abundance of the things which he possesseth" (Luke 12:15).

Living life from the outside to the inside does not afford an individual the possibility of developing an internal values system which is based upon intellectual integrity, moral character and spiritual understanding. Unfortunately, Christian leadership mentality has encouraged the valuing of tangibles (things) rather than intangibles (moral character, intellectual integrity, and spiritual understanding). On Sunday, October 23, 2016 in Sumter, South Carolina, in St. Paul A.M.E. church one parishioner violently stabbed another parishioner during worship services. In the twenty-first century, individuals cannot attend church and worship God in spirit and truth without being subject to potentially losing one's life. Hebrews 2:3 says, "How shall we escape, if we neglect so great salvation; which at first began to be spoken by the Lord, and was confirmed unto us by them that heard him…" Romans 10:10 tells us, "For with the heart man believeth unto righteousness; and with the mouth confession is made unto salvation."

The challenges of creative living in a spiritually dying, sin-sick culture of having or not having the material creature comforts of the American dream are much easier to face when individuals have their spiritual lifestyles in order. The missing moral links in the family structure and Christian leadership mentalities are the sources of the problems destroying American culture. Culture is not god. Even though, religion and culture can invariably become one culture Christianity monument building.

Society begins and ends in family structure, and when the family structure deteriorates, society spiritually and morally declines. To be sure, in the twenty-first century, American families are recycling dysfunctional spiritual curses from generation to generation. Family life relationships are the foundation for moral character development. Life is about character development. The David and King Saul saga was about moral character development (First Samuel 24). King Saul had been hunting David to kill him. David could have killed King Saul, but he rose above the code of "an eye for an eye and a tooth for a tooth." When Saul finally met

David face to face, he saw himself for what he really was and he broke down, lifted up his voice and wept, "Thou art more righteous than I, for thou hast rewarded me good, whereas I have rewarded thee evil" (First Samuel 24:17). Great is the individual that rules his own spirit or mind because greater is he that rules his own spirit than he who takes a city.

Character development is about spiritual and moral values, and the valuing of people rather than valuing things and the pleasure principle. American society is in dire need of the spiritual and moral integration of flesh and spirit. But, just like Pilate, too many Americans have washed their hands in despair, called it quits, and said let the record stand. Yes, we may always have institutional racism, sexism, classism and socio-economic injustice because there will always be those who are not willing to set positive moral examples of character and intellectual integrity for others to imitate. It is primarily for this reason that America has a 2016 presidential election of moral confusion. It is unfortunate that a few rich and powerful individuals or able to morally influence the many into going in the wrong direction spiritually, morally, and culturally. The classic example of this problem is the way Donald Trump has so easily misled millions of Americans into the false hope of acquiring something for nothing. America, "We are troubled on every side, yet not distressed; we are perplexed, but not in despair; persecuted but not forsaken; cast down, but not destroyed" (2 Corinthians 4:8-9). Selah!

16

ONE IN GOD, AND ALL IN CHRIST

In order to minimize confusion, because confusion is of the devil, and the devil's desire is to confuse every individual. "For God is not the author of confusion, but of peace, as in all churches of the saints" (1 Corinthians 14:33). The social sources of denominationalism, as well as, the over fifty different versions of the Bible in print might be the cause of "devilish" spiritual confusion in Christian churches, not God. God is not confused.

However, in all Christian denominations there are several universal truths that transcend denominationalism: The Holy Trinity (God the Three in One: God the father, God the Son, and God the Holy Spirit), and Holy Baptism. "For God so loved the world, that he gave his only begotten Son, that whosoever believeth in him should not perish, but have everlasting life" (John 3:16). However, every individual ought to thoroughly, and completely understand this spiritual truth: "But without faith it is impossible to please him: for he that cometh to God must believe that he is, and that he is a rewarder of them that diligently seek him" (Hebrews 11:6). This scriptural verse is precisely what salvation and being born again is all about.

We all know that teaching and preaching the Word of God from any Biblical source based upon a godly desire to do good-works oriented toward loving and serving others is admirable, because

God loves and serves everyone. Christians: We are one in God, and therefore, why not one Biblical source (Bible)? Christian believers, we are Christians, simply because Christ first loved and served us. And, we are called to be Christ-like by loving and serving each other in Jesus's name, a "peculiar-people." So, "Let this mind be in you, which was also in Christ Jesus: who being in the form of God, thought it not robbery to be equal to God: but made himself of no reputation, and took upon him the form of a servant, and was made in the likeness of men: and being found in the fashion as a man, he humbled himself, and became obedient unto death, even the death of the cross" (Philippians 2: 5-8).

Question: How do Christians achieve a spiritual walk with God, and a spiritual talk in Christ? There is only one way to achieve spiritual clarity in God, from pulpits to the pews, and that is by Christians "reading" the same Biblical source for instruction in the Will of God, and revelatory knowledge. Both pastors, as well as, parishioners must go through the same Christian "spiritual" process in order to receive salvation, and be spiritually born again. No individual, even Jesus's mother, could escape the spiritual-reality of this scripture. "For we must all appear before the judgment seat of Christ: that every one may receive the things done in his body, according to that he hath done, whether it be good or bad" (2 Corinthians 5:10). There are a lot of ways that this spiritual truth can be stated, and behold here's another way. "So then every one of us shall give account of himself to God" (Romans 14:12). We are all in the same boat. Therefore, "peace be still", because God is no respecter of personalities and positions.

Of course, let's make no mistake about it; we need pastoral leaders. The Bible says, "How then shall they call on him in whom they have not believed? And how shall they believe in him of whom they have not heard? And how shall they preach, except they are sent? As it is written, How beautiful are the feet of them that preach the gospel of peace, and bring glad tidings of good things!" (Romans 10:14-15).

This is why God desires that all of us, pastors and parishioners alike, "Be sober, be vigilant, because your adversary the devil, as a roaring lion, walketh about, seeking whom he may devour: whom resist stedfast in the faith, knowing that the same afflictions are accomplished in your brethren that are in the world" (1 Peter 5:8-9).

There is a profound spiritual question that all of us must ask, and all of us sooner or later must answer, and that is: "How shall we escape, if we neglect so great salvation; which at the first began to be spoken by the Lord, and was confirmed unto us by them that heard him..." (Hebrews 2:3).

Question: Why do men of God use so many different Bibles? Is it simply because if a spiritual misinterpretation is spoken from the pulpit then parishioners would not know the contextual error? Or is it because of the same set of socio-spiritual-circumstances associated with denominationalism which causes division, strife and confusion in Christianity?

There are over fifty different versions of the Bible. Questions: Why are there so many different versions of the Bible? Why do different Christian denominations prefer different versions of the Bible? These are questions that all Christian believers should ask.

Readers will note that this god-fearing editorial writer always uses the King James Version of the Bible for several reasons. The primary reason is that most Christians possess and use the King James Version. In fact, the "greatest generation" read the King James Version. Maybe this is why the "greatest generation" was not spiritually confused. Of course, The King James Version was commissioned by King James of England in the 1600s and transcribed by men of God. Therefore, all praises to God for this "inspired version" of the Bible based upon original manuscripts. The other reason why I prefer using The King James Bible is because it requires quality "spiritual-study" time with God in order that the Holy Spirit might inform readers of original "contextual" intent that is revelatory truth: "God is a Spirit: and they that worship him must worship him in spirit and in truth" (John 4:24). Selah!

17

Partisan Politics: Public Policy

Thank God for the two-party political system. But, unfortunately, rather than becoming diplomatically adversarial in terms of what is good for America; the two-party political system has evolved into un-statesmen-like partisan politics, cultural and ethnic discrimination, and closed-mindedness. God created all nations to dwell upon the face of the earth in peace and unity. If you live by the sword you die by the sword (Matthew 26:52, Isaiah 2:4).

The presidential election of 2016 is a watershed moment in American political history: Which way, America? Chaos or national unity? Questions: Whatever happened to compassionate conservatism? Or the angelic side of points of light rather than devilish greed? In the twenty-first century, seemingly the darker side of devilish selfishness is prevailing rather than moral civility.

How did we arrive at this crossroad in American political history? It has always been said that politics is about the future, and of course, the future belongs to our children and future generations. The question is: Who will pay for the future? The answer is our children; simply because there are no free rides, even though frugality should be observed at all times. Freedom is not free, and stagnation is undesirable, because economic stagnation can turn into inflation, and inflation can become depression. And, when the middle class is out of work, and the issue of too-big-to-fail becomes public policy then economic chaos ensues.

Again, the question is: What has happened to the American Dream and our democratic political system? Has it gone to the dawn of a bright and blissful new morning or has it slipped into the eternal deep dark pit of midnight? Spiritually-oriented political leadership can resolve the governance dilemma facing American society. In the words of Rodney King, "Can we all just get along?" And, of course, President Abraham Lincoln said it best: "A nation divided against itself cannot stand." Both political parties are dividing Americans into socio-economic-political camps, rather than unifying Americans as Americans. Unfortunately, this is especially true of one particular political Party. Both Rodney King's and Abraham Lincoln's statements ring loud, true, and profoundly clear in the twenty-first century; especially given the nonsensical-rancor in the 2016 presidential election. This is the message that all Americans should clearly hear: "God is light, and in him is no darkness at all, If we say that we have fellowship with him, and walk in darkness, we lie, and do not the truth: but if we walk in the light, as he is in the light, we have fellowship one with another, and the blood of Jesus Christ his Son cleanseth us from all sin" (1 John 1:5-7).

With good spiritual leadership in our families, churches, educational institutions, and political party system, we can overcome the potentially disastrous tsunami headed our way, that is, if we heed the Word of God. "Nevertheless when it shall turn to the Lord, the veil shall be taken away. Now the Lord is that Spirit: and where the Spirit of the Lord is, there is liberty" (2 Corinthians 3:16-17).

This socio-spiritual-commentary is like unto John the Baptist crying in the wilderness of spiritual ignorance: Repent! Repent! Repent! "He that hath an ear, let him hear what the Spirit saith unto the churches; He that overcometh shall not be hurt of the second death" (Revelation 4:11).

What God has done in this great nation called America, no individual or group of individuals because of their unadulterated power-seeking, envy, unbridled greed, and perverted lustful desires, should put asunder.

Truly, America, let's just all get along, and agree with sound Biblical doctrine. "If two of you shall agree on earth as touching anything that they shall ask, it shall be done for them of my Father which is in Heaven. For where two or three are gathered together in my name, there am I in the midst of them" (Matthew 18:19-20). Know this, America, any nation divided against itself because of ethnic and cultural status differentiations cannot stand.

We do not need any type or form of new declarations, because we all know that there is nothing new under the sun (Ecclesiastes 1:9), but from time to time we need to be reminded by the Great I Am. "Brethren, I write no new commandment unto you, but an old commandment which ye had from the beginning" (1 John 2:7).

As Americans, we have a moral charge to live up to the discipline of our own moral conscience, and the spiritual words as recorded and agreed to in the preamble to the *U.S. Constitution*: "We hold these truths to be self-evident that all men are created equal, that they are endowed by their creator with certain inalienable rights, and among these are life, liberty, and the pursuit of happiness." The *U.S. Constitution* is almost a perfectly written governing document. It is a document that the world had never seen before, because it included everyone as equal members of society. Unfortunately, the legal enforcement of the document is mired in race/ethnicity, social class, and gender discrimination. This is why the nature of the American dilemma is both spiritual as well as socio-economic. We do not have racism by law, but racism exists in individual mind-sets and institutional power resources. This is why Americans must make a concerted spiritual effort to get it right with God, and keep it right for future generations. Then and only then can we get it right in our families, churches, and educational institutions. Selah!

18
POLITICS AND STRANGE BED PARTNERS

Donald Trump has embarked upon a scorch societal policy. If I cannot become the president, then I will destroy American society as we know it. Without a doubt, the Trumpster already knows that he has discredited himself as a presidential candidate. And, as a result, America's international image is tainted due to Trump's uncivil behavior. His statement in the third debate is positive proof of his self-centered destructive mentality when he refused to say that he would accept the final results of the 2016 presidential election. Now, the Trumpeter is flaming the fires of vigilantism. Just like Nero, Trump is playing on his harp based upon his privileged birth position while helping to bring America to her knees internally by sowing seeds of doubt in free, fair, and just elections. Unfortunately, the day after the debate the Trumpster added fuel to the fire by saying, "I'll accept the results, if **I** win." This is the big "I" in the middle of sin.

Trump is manipulating non-college-educated white males whose jobs have been sent abroad by profiteering businessmen just like Trump, whose only concern is bottom-line profits, not American families. Yet, these same working class White males have been hood-winked into believing that it is trade policy agreements that have created the economic problem of loss of living wage jobs, not corporate greed. Working class White males need to change their spiritual and political mind-set. "I beseech you therefore, brethren, by the mercies of God, that ye present your bodies a living sacrifice, holy, acceptable unto God, which is your reasonable service. And be not conformed to this world, but be ye transformed by the renewing of your mind, that ye may prove what is that good, acceptable, and perfect, will of God" (Romans 12:1-2).

Trump followers, when you choose an extremely flawed presidential standard-bearer such as the Trumpster you have placed your children's children's lives in the balance, because they will never be able to realize the American Dream. Therefore, look at the individual in the mirror, and spiritually understand this scripture: "When he speaketh fair, believe him not: for there are seven abominations in his heart." The Biblical reference is to the the seven deadly sins ("a proud look, a lying tongue, hands that shed innocent blood, a heart that deviseth wicked imaginations, feet that are swift to run to mischief, a false witness that speaketh lies, and he that soweth discord among brethren"). Of course, sin is lawlessness and vanity. And, "Whose hatred is covered by deceit, his wickedness shall be shewed before the whole congregation" (The World: Saturday, October 7, 2016; Proverbs 26: 25-26). The spirit of Abraham Lincoln is probably grieved at what has happened to the Republican Party as the spiritual backbone of freedom, justice, and equality of opportunity for all Americans.

Donald Trump in his own words has told the world in no uncertain, undignified what he thinks of women, immigrants, and other Americans. Every woman is a potential mother, and should be treated with the highest regards and respect. Therefore, I do not need to remind anyone of the spiritual-biological factor associated with motherhood. And, likewise, every man is a potential father. All Americans are duty-called to make America live up to the Preamble of the *U.S. Constitution.* Thus, let every American pray to our Heavenly Father (GOD); especially Christian Right Evangelicals that most fathers do not spiritually and politically imitate the behavior of the Trumpster, because we all know that Esau tricked his brother Jacob out of his birthright. When all is said and done, all individuals need to "spiritually" understand this scripture; especially the Trumpster: "He that keepeth his mouth keepeth his life: but he that openeth wide his lips shall have destruction" (Proverbs 13:3).

The Trumpster has boldly said from his own mouth who he is; a sexual predator, hater of minority immigrants and fellow Americans who are not fortunate enough to be born to rich parents. By the way, we also hope and pray that potential mothers are not chasing after rainbows looking for a pot of gold that is searching for something for nothing (gold diggers). We all know that nothing from nothing leaves nothing. Individuals should not judge, but should always try the Spirit by the Spirit; therefore, there is a possibility that the Donald is not capable of receiving redemption.

The Trumpster with his unfounded malicious allegations (habitual lying) that the 2016 presidential election is "rigged" is stroking the embers of ungodly societal violence, and at the same time, playing on the frustrations of weak minded individuals who are capable of committing criminal acts. Of course, no other presidential election has been rigged. It's all about him! Stupid! Stupid! Stupid! Why wasn't the 2008 presidential election rigged against President Obama (birther movement)? And why wasn't the 2000 election rigged against President George W. Bush since the Democratic Party was in charge of the White House? The answer to the question is simply this: In American society there is a check on the checker, and above all, both political parties believe in the time honored tradition of fair and just democratic elections. But, more importantly, both political parties believe in a smooth transition of power. (Just ask "gentleman" presidential candidate Al Gore).

Donald Trump has no political leadership history that the American people can judge and evaluate him by. But, what he does have is a selfish business record that all Americans can evaluate and inspect, because it includes six business bankruptcies, including one for almost one billion dollars. What kind of hooking/crooking businessman is this, because even with other people's money he fails? This is why the American people deserve to see his federal income tax returns. One thing we do know about the "Trumpster" in his business ventures, has left a lot of individuals holding what elephants leave on fairgrounds. Trump supporters, wake up, embrace commonsense reality, and ask God's forgiveness for being so naively gullible before it is too late. Finally, Christian right evangelicals meditate on this Scripture, because "Trumpster" has built some buildings with other people's money, but "For every house is builded by some man, but He that built all things is God" (Hebrews 3:4). Our earnest prayer is that America never forgets it. Selah!

19

Religious Conservatism versus All White Conservatism

To be or not to be is an eternal question because it is a question about commitment that is children of God versus children of Cain: Who is on the Lord's side? Without a doubt, "Before destruction the heart of man is haughty, and before honour is humility" (Proverbs 18:12). But, more importantly, "Death and life are in the power of the tongue" (Proverbs 18:21). All individuals, especially individuals who are seeking high profile public leadership positions like that of the presidency of the United States of America (multi-cultural society), should choose their words wisely. Because "There is a way which seemeth right unto a man, but the end thereof are the ways of death" (Proverbs 14:12). "For God is not the author of confusion, but of peace, as in all the churches of the saints" (1 Corinthians 14: 33). Therefore, children of God do not create confusion, because all things must be done decently and in order; especially in a democratic society.

If a want to be leader cannot live by this Holy Scripture, "But grow in grace, and in the knowledge of our Lord and Savior Jesus Christ. To Him be glory both now and forever" (2 Peter 3:18), he or she does not qualify as a want to be leader.

The Trump phenomenon is primarily grounded in white working class misunderstanding and racial and ethnic socio-economic scapegoating. In fact, the Trump presidential candidacy has exposed the ugly white privilege underbelly of the Republican Party, as well as, the hypocrisy of American society as a democratic melting pot. Of course, the socio-economic failures of white working class Americans have nothing whatsoever to do with the existence of permanent tan minorities in America. The system is rigged based upon the principle of white privilege and institutional racism. And, by the way, trade agreements have little or nothing to do with the loss of skill level jobs, but everything to do with the financial bottom line of multinational corporations and enterprises, not federal trade policies. This is why individuals need an education in a democratic technological information society. By the way, individuals with guns do not alleviate the problem or the conditions of jobs going abroad. Neither does same-sex marriage create jobs, only societal confusion because "Righteousness exalteth a nation, but sin is a reproach to any people" (Proverbs 14:34). But, we all should know, "For as he thinketh in his heart, so is he" (Proverbs 23:7).

Therefore, working class whites need to stop whining, stop looking for privileges based upon skin color in a multicultural nation, stop following leaders with immoral and psychological challenges, obtain occupational retraining, obtain a quality education, and by and large, meaningful employment is available.

Nevertheless, when it is all said and done, all of us sin, and come short of the glory of God. "And as it is appointed unto men once to die, but after this the judgment" (Hebrews 9:27). Indeed, it is unfortunate that, "Fools make a mock at sin, but among the righteous there is favour" (Proverbs 14:9). And, above all, God-fearing Americans understand that, "The wisdom of the prudent is to understand His (God's) way, but the folly of fools is deceit" (Proverbs 14:8).

Most individuals are conservative based upon spiritual principles, moral values, and conscience. However, Republican conservatism has evolved into white paranoia. In fact, it is Biblically recorded that God made a man out of dirt, and breathed into his nostrils the breath of life. The last time I checked there is no such element as white dirt. Therefore, life and death issues are not grounded in skin color, but the will of God (Matthew 22:36-40).

All white conservatism is the only rational explanation for the rise of a Donald Trump leadership style personality bold enough to seek the presidency of supposedly the most sophisticated democratic nation-state in the world community? The Republican Party is an original major political party whose founding personality and godly spirit was Abraham Lincoln: "Together we stand, divided we fall." In fact, the party of Lincoln was established on the time honored principle of justice and liberty for all, not all white conservatism. It is, indeed, an unfortunate set of circumstances for America (a nation of immigrants), as well as, the world community that the Republican Party since 1964 (Senator Barry Goldwater) has been marching toward a Donald Trump style presidency.

Whites rule the world, but God rules the universe, and minorities do have a say in how whites govern, especially in American society because of the power of the vote. Just maybe this is why voting rights is under legal attack by all white conservatism. Of course, at one time in America's history voting rights were under attack both legally, as well as, physically. The right to vote is the cornerstone sacred principle of participatory democracy. Therefore, thank God for President Lyndon B. Johnson and the Civil Rights Act 1964 and the Voting Rights Act 1965.

As Americans, we must right the ship of state, spiritually correct the course, and "Let us therefore come boldly unto the throne of grace, that we may obtain mercy, and find grace to help in time of need" (Hebrews 4:16).

20

DON'T SELL OUT THE AMERICAN DREAM

Voting for Trump is selling-out the American dream, the inheritance of your offspring, as well as, the aspirations of future generations of Americans. Trump has gamed the system and hoodwinked working class whites. Conservatives tend to be extremely hard on welfare system cheaters, but yet are willing to give Trump a pass on business venture exploitation against small businesses and tax cheating. Wake up America, especially Black Americans. Life is too short to be stupid. Life does not exist in material things (Luke 12:15). The Republican Party was indeed naïve and insensitive to American values and the American dream. But, America are we so completely confused as to elect to the office of the presidency an unhinged man who is not capable of making moral decisions and understanding what it means to be the leader of the free world? Yet, on the other hand, he admires the world's most prominent dictator: Putin. And, more importantly, disrespects the leader of the free world, President Barack Obama, disrespects mothers (women), disrespects an entire ethnic Hispanic culture, contractually and financially cheats some small business contractors, and has gamed the tax system for eighteen years. A so-called spiritual minded individual does not collect charitable funds from others and then uses those funds on perpetuating and glorifying himself.

Does avoiding paying taxes make an individual a genius? Some high profile political leaders think so. However, Jesus Christ and the Bible have a vastly different perspective. According to Jesus paying your taxes is a moral duty. The Pharisees (religious hypocrites) plotted to entangle Jesus by asking this question. Christian right evangelicals, as well as other believers, in the business genius of Donald Trump receive the truth of this scriptural message, "Tell us therefore, what thinkest thou? Is it lawful to give tribute unto Caesar, or not? But Jesus perceived their wickedness, and said, Why tempt ye me, ye hypocrites? Shew me the tribute money. And they brought unto him a penny. And he saith unto to them, Whose is this image and superscription? They said unto him, Caesar's. Then saith he unto them, Render therefore unto Caesar the things which are Caesar's, and unto God the things that are God's. When they had heard these words, they marveled, and left him, and went their way" (Matthew 22:17-22).

Trump, genius political followers of Trump, Christian right evangelicals, and others heed the unadulterated Word of God. Christian right evangelicals stop admiring the wealth of a man and understand his moral character (Christ-like qualities). Money is not God. Money is a tool and should be used as such, not used as a fool. The presidential candidacy of Trump has exposed the underbelly of American society, and in so doing, exampled before the world that America is just as vulnerable to demagoguery as any other nation-state: Hitlerism, Mussolinism, Communism, and the modern-day likes of Putinism. The Trump presidential candidacy has revealed more about who America is than what it is that Donald Trump can do as president. Trump supporters you have been played with very little intellectual integrity and moral accountability because the Trump family business auxiliaries have been paid almost nine million dollars from public campaign funds. Trump has told everyone that his business philosophy is use other people's money for personal gain, and he tries very hard to never spend his own money.

Do you want Trump spending your tax dollars? Trump has told America he does not pay taxes, but he loves the military services system that protects him. He loves the highway system he is chauffeured on, the friendly skies (air traffic system) that his private plane flies in, and I could go on and on. However, Trump wants your tax dollars to pay for those services and not his. Shame! Shame! Shame! Without a doubt, Trump says that he is a very successful businessman, but we will never know the truth unless we see his tax returns. Show your tax returns because most Americans believe in the Reagan doctrine: Trust, but verify! However, we do know that Trump is a pro at hooking and crooking and using other people's money.

The American dream has become the American nightmare; especially for many working class white males. Even for some white Americans with college degrees obtaining the American dream is a difficult proposition, because of the greed of multinational corporations and the outsourcing of jobs overseas. This socio-economic fact of American society is what propelled the Bernie Sanders presidential campaign, that is, the inability of many millennium whites to obtain college degrees, as well as, meaningful employment opportunities, not federal governmental trade agreements. In the nineteenth and twentieth centuries the American dream was based primarily upon white males completing high school, obtaining a union factory based job which afforded the ability to purchase a home, buy a car, provide a college education for their children, and obtain excellent retirement benefits. Those days are "Gone with the Wind." The Twenty-first century has become a system based upon technological advances, computers, robots, and machines that are more cost effective and productive than human labor capital. This process has produced the angry white male syndrome because human labor is cheaper overseas than in America. Just ask Donald Trump, because he has shipped his human labor jobs overseas.

Trump and his loyal supporters should stop scapegoating on Blacks, religious groups, and other minorities. Your lack of success is not caused by the existence of minorities in American society. Jobs are controlled primarily by white men, even white women are in electronic slavery, because they have institutional difficulties obtaining equal pay for equal work. This is why affirmative action set asides include white women as a minority group. Even though, if the truth be told, white women are the majority, living in the same house, and at the same time, sleeping with the problem. What a high level Trump campaign official stated concerning Blacks is more applicable to whites. Allow me to paraphrase: "If a white individual is unsuccessful in America; it is truly because you are lazy, and therefore, you have no one to earthly blame but yourself."

It seems as though the Trump campaign is fueled by the desire on the part of some whites to recolonize Blacks economically, and at the same time, bring back the southern Confederacy mentality that is the glory days of white privilege (white cultural superiority). America have faith, but not in a Trump. "Finally, brethren, whatsoever things are true, whatsoever things are honest, whatsoever things are just, whatsoever things are pure, whatsoever things are lovely, whatsoever things are of good report: if there be any virtue, and if there be any praise, think on these things" (Philippians 4:6-8). Selah!

21

THE AFTERMATH: A NATION DIVIDED

President Abraham Lincoln said it best, "A nation divided against itself cannot stand." President-elect Donald J. Trump employed hateful divisive language in order to ascend to the presidency. The 2016 presidential election employed hate-speech, xenophobia, religious bigotry, and bullying. And everything that was wrong with America was initiated by President Barack Obama as the worst President in America's history. But, more importantly, only President Donald J. Trump can fix it. Every American should respect the office of president, and above all, the peaceful political transfer of power from one individual to another. Even though it is extremely difficult to forget the hateful rhetoric of President-elect Trump.

President-elect Donald Trump is who America has been (past), who America is (present), and who America desires to be in the future. The why of the election of Donald Trump was an unhealthy response to multi-culturalism that is the tanning of American society (a just society). The what were the invisible "For White Only" signs brightly mentally shining in white mentality and behavioral patterns. "For as he thinketh in his heart so is he" (Proverbs 23:7). Many whites clearly displayed what they think about minorities when they sought to discredit the legitimate election of President Obama in 2008 with the birther movement" spearheaded by the Trumpster. Additionally, the 2016 presidential election of Donald J. Trump is likening unto the people choosing Barabbas over Jesus. Minorities beware you do not have a place at America's table, because the concept of one nation under God with liberty and justice for all was not elected to the office of president on November 8th, 2016. Beware of train cattle cars on side-tracks in your communities because President-elect Trump has promised to ship 11 million undocumented workers back to their countries of origin. We needed your manual labor services for a short while. Now, your manual labor services are no longer needed, because you are the source of our problem. Even the world now knows that the problem in American society is white privilege. Allies (NATO) beware of both the Bear and the Bald Eagle. For now we all know that the 2016 presidential election was grounded in a toxic sense of white privilege. Too many whites want more white privilege and more privileges abundantly.

Maybe there is a desire on the part of some whites to "Make America Great Again" by reestablishing a slave state mentality for minority groups. While, on the other hand, the majority of minorities desire the best for whites, but not to their own detriment. Even though minorities in the twenty-first century are the last hired and the first fired.

Is the election of Donald J. Trump to the office of presidency Custer's last stand for institutional racism? For without a doubt, if individuals spiritually know better they should exemplify a better understanding of what they know. Whites in electing Donald Trump have shown minorities that their only concern is white privilege. Donald Trump said that he could shoot someone on Madison Avenue and whites would continue to support him. This is the presidential leadership mentality of the leader of the free world. Leadership is about internal values, not external trappings. It is truly amazing that so many college educated and economically successful whites voted for this kind of leadership mentality. And Trump has surrounded himself with the same type of leadership mentality.

Our NATO allies soon and very soon will evaluate America's leadership position in the world community. In so doing, they will probably conclude that Putin presents himself as Donald Trump has declared a better leader than President Obama; therefore, NATO's best interest might be to form an alliance with Russia, and why not?

What will be the role of the loyal opposition (Democratic Party)? Do we end up in federal governmental gridlock? This is precisely what happened with a Democratic president and a Republican controlled Senate and House of Representatives. Now, we have two branches (Presidency and the Legislative) of the federal government controlled by the Republicans.

Will the outcome be positive for all Americans? The Democratic Party must fight for socio-economic inclusion and cultural fairness for all Americans. If the Democratic Party relents and does not fight for justice and inclusion for all Americans then they may as well become Republicans because they will not receive overwhelming minority support again. To be sure, informed citizens understand that the very social nature of political democracy requires positive compromises. This is why democracy requires a spiritually enlightened and educated citizenry because democracy is not just about money. Dictatorship is my way, not the highway, but death.

Democracy is for an intelligent citizenry; therefore, college students get ready for decreases in educational federal funding because the Ryan budget decimates educational funding for college students. Does it really matter? Because in the end the formally educated, the formally uneducated, the elderly, as well as the spiritually ignorant, all voted for a spiritually dysfunctional leadership mentality.

On November 10th, 2016, President-elect Donald J. Trump and President Barack Obama met in the Oval Office of the White House for an hour and a half. President-elect Trump superficially appeared to momentarily act presidential.

Can a skunk change his disdaining odor? "When he speaketh fair, believe him not: for there are seven abominations in his heart. Whose hatred is covered by deceit, his wickedness shall be shewed before the whole congregation. Whoso diggeth a pit shall fall therein: and he that rolleth a stone, it will return upon him. A lying tongue hateth those that are afflicted by it; and a flattering mouth worketh ruin" (Proverbs 26:25-28). This Scripture says it all, "Be not deceived; God is not mocked: for whatsoever a man soweth, that he shall also reap. For he that soweth to his flesh shall of his flesh reap corruption; but he that soweth to the Spirit shall of the Spirit reap everlasting life. And let us not be weary in well doing: for in due season we shall reap, if we faint not" (Galatians 6:7-8).

America, God is watching you. Take heed, "For the Lord is great, and greatly to be praise" (Psalms 96:4). For after all is said and done, rich or poor, "There is no wisdom nor understanding nor counsel against the Lord" (Proverbs 21:30). Love overcomes hatred. Selah!

22

THE HOODWINKING OF WORKING CLASS WHITE MALES

On November 8th, 2016, many white working class males, who are uneducated and unsophisticated, will not vote for Donald Trump. Or they will simply stay at home and not vote at all. Even those working class white males who support Trump understand that his leadership style is about madness. Donald Trump cannot discipline his own tongue because, "If any man among you seem to be religious, and bridleth not his tongue, but deceiveth his own heart, this man's religion is vain" (James 1:26). Godly Americans know that life and death are in the tongue and therefore, "A double minded man is unstable in all of his ways" (James 1:8). But more importantly, "Keep thy tongue from evil, and thy lips from speaking guile. Depart from evil, and do good: seek peace, and pursue it" (Psalm 34:13-14). In fact, most supporters of Donald Trump know that he is intellectually unfit and emotionally unstable and should not hold the office of president. But more importantly, they know that it would be disastrous for their families, their loved ones, their neighbors, their friends, and above all, the nation that we all love, these United States of America. Supporters of Trump you might hate the messenger, even hate this message, but you should love the sanctified truth; thus, O Lord, "Sanctify them through thy truth: thy word is truth" (John 17:17).

"The man that wandereth out of the way of understanding shall remain in the congregation of the dead" (Proverbs 21:16). Life is about personal responsibility that is knowing how to become a living sacrifice to God, not the world. Believe me, Donald Trump has absolutely no clue concerning this Scripture of inspiration, "I beseech you therefore, brethren, by the mercies of God, that ye present your bodies a living sacrifice, holy, acceptable unto God, which is your reasonable service. And be not conformed to this world: but be ye transformed by the renewing of your mind, that ye may prove what is that good, and acceptable, and perfect will of God" (Romans 12:1-2).

If anyone can reason with Donald Trump, ask him to pray or even pray with him, and read this scripture as spiritual inspiration, "Thy word have I hid in mine heart, that I might not sin against thee" (Psalms 119:11). Also read Luke 12:15, "Take heed, and beware of covetousness: for a man's life consisteth not in the abundance of the things which he possesseth." Donald Trump may not know this, but his soul weighs in the balance; therefore, read and heed, "For what shall it profit a man, if he shall gain the whole world, and lose his own soul?" (Mark 8:36). Republican evangelical leaders, why aren't you bringing these Scriptures of inspirations to the heart and mind of Donald Trump? God is no respecter of person and He created all of us for His glory. Therefore, "Thou art worthy, O Lord, to receive glory and honour and power: for thou hast created all things, and for thy pleasure they are and were created" (Revelation 4:11).

The will of God is that individuals love others as they love themselves (the second of the Great Commandments, Matthew 22:39). We cannot question whether or not Donald Trump or any other individual loves God because that is personal in nature, between God and the individual. But we can say emphatically and without a doubt, Donald Trump does not love America's neighbor, Mexico. However, there are two additional things we know that Trump does love: himself and money. One could be a sin; however, God is the only one who can judge who Trump loves more, God or himself (Psalms 7:11). The love of money is most definitely a sin because the Bible clearly states, "For the love of money is the root of all evil: which while some coveted after, they have erred from the faith, and pierced themselves through with many sorrows" (1 Timothy 6:10).

Donald Trump is a chronic, habitual liar and lying is a sin (Ten Commandments). God hates a liar, that is a lying tongue. In fact, bearing false witness against one's neighbor is a cardinal sin because, "When he speaketh a lie, he speaketh of his own: for he is a liar..." (John 8:44). Donald Trump's life has been one of personal gain, not public service to fellow Americans. A Godly leader knows how to love and serve in Jesus' name, not seek to be served and self-glorified as though, "I am the only one that can fix it. I know more than the Generals."

This election is truly a watershed election for the heart and soul of American society, as well as the ability of Americans to live out the true spiritual meaning of the creed embodied in the U.S. Constitution, the preamble, and the Declaration of Independence, "We hold these truths to be self-evident that all men are created equal, and endowed by their Creator without certain inalienable rights"

The worst thing to potentially come out of Donald Trump becoming the standard bearer of the Grand Ole Party is the utter demise of the reputation of the party of Lincoln. The standard bearer of a major political party should never internally splinter the party, that is, be given the power to drive a wedge between members of the party as well as the American people. "Humpty Dumpty sat on the wall, and Humpty Dumpty had a great fall." And all of the political movers and shakers were not able to put the party back together again. Republicans, get it together; you have your work cut out for you because it will be a monumental task restoring the party of Lincoln. It has been said that in order to have a great democracy, a great society must have educated individuals (voters) in order to make intelligent decisions, rather than emotional decisions. Donald Trump is a nightmare, a joke gone horribly bad for American society. Some Americans are simply confused, but most Americans are bewildered by the very thought of a Trump presidency. For without a doubt, individuals who are supporting Trump for the office of president are uneducated, misguided, emotionally bankrupt, and above all, seeking white privilege. Without a doubt, Trump is insulting the intelligence of white working class males by talking loud and saying nothing.

Believe it or not, at one point in time, most Blacks were Republican. What happened? America needs a loyal, two-party political opposition system, especially for governmental policy check and balances. America, we are in a horrible mess, but, "If my people, which are called by my name, shall humble themselves, and pray, and seek my face, and turn from their wicked ways; then will I hear from heaven, and will forgive their sin, and will heal their land" (2 Chronicle 7:14). Selah!

23
THE SYSTEM

It has rightly been said, the system works for the designers of the system, rather than individual citizens. Without a doubt, a society can make anything legal or illegal if it so desires, but is it moral is the deeper spiritual question. Designers of a societal structure can add, subtract, and divide, even rewrite tenets in order to ensure that the structure of society always benefits them (the designers). Social scientists have traditionally declared that American society is the melting pot of the world community (melting pot theory). Of course, Blacks were never in the socio-economic concept of the melting pot theory. If Blacks were in the melting pot then the pot would neither be white nor Black, but tan or brown (biological extinction). In fact, Blacks have never been a part of the so called melting pot theoretical structure, but always targets (profiled) by a system of totem pole discrimination" racial and ethnic injustice. Blacks are at the bottom of the totem pole that is in a static position, rather than given constitutional civil rights (social mobility opportunities).

When will Blacks be treated fairly by the system, even though Blacks are legal citizens? Blacks are rarely if ever treated legally fair by the system, because of the racial makeup of the system (power-brokers). But, God. It was God that delivered the Israelites from bondage in Egypt (Exodus 12:33-51). It was God that saved Paul and Silas from their unjust incarceration, because they were teaching and preaching God's Word (Acts 16:22-40). And it was the strong will of Blacks to pull themselves out of the pit of slavery into the will and mercy of God which saved Blacks in America since 1619 (Plymouth Rock), with the help of some fair-minded white men. Jesus said no one is good but God.

The history and development of the policing system in the United States is closely aligned to the system in England. America's system of organized policing is more than 385 years old commencing after 1630, which in turn, allowed local ordinances to be enacted establishing a constable appointment system for neighborhood patrolling. The American judicial system was designed to protect white males and their property rights, and white females were considered as property (e.g., miscegenation laws). Another key component of law enforcement has always been keeping minorities check-mated (denial of constitutional civil rights). The denial of constitutional rights (civil liberties) was through profiling, intimidation and murder. The majority of Americans gave consent through silence. Silence is not golden, but yellow without moral conscience. Therefore, policing in American society is in dire need of a professional attitude adjustment because attitudes influence behavior.

Some of the original framers of the governing document (preamble to the U.S. Constitution) spiritually attempted to stay the course and keep the faith by instituting a mass universal educational system. Primarily for two reasons: (1) democracy requires an educated citizenry; and (2) democracy requires spiritual enlightenment, that is, the ability of individuals to read the Bible with spiritual understanding and moral clarity (Revelation 1:3). Bible is an acronym for B=basic, I=instruction, B=before, L=leaving, E=earth. All individuals die regardless of race, creed, or skin color, because all of us know, "And as it is appointed unto men once to die, but after this the judgment" (Hebrews 9:27).

Heavenly Father, we all understand that your Word is settled in Heaven (Psalms 119:89). But more importantly, we all know that "God judgeth the righteous, and God is angry with the wicked every day" (Psalms 7:11). God hates sin (Proverbs 6:16). Individuals love sinning because there are benefits in sinning. Otherwise individuals would not sin. Jesus said it best,: "For by thy words thou shalt be justified, and by thy words thou shalt be condemned" (Matthew 12: 37).

It has primarily been the executive branch of the American political system that has to some degree kept our heads above water (adult at the table), because the judicial and legislative branches of our governmental system are confused concerning power and its uses. These branches of our governmental system are acting just like little children, who declare that "it is my way or the highway." Without understanding that the spiritual righteousness of a nation is weighing in the balance because, "Righteousness exalteth a nation, but sin is a reproach to any people" (Proverbs 14:34).

The Biblical influence on the U.S. Constitution and the lofty spiritual tenets of the system are now being made null and void because of secular humanism and the social fact that the legislative branch of our governmental system is completely without a spiritual moral compass. And the U.S. Supreme Court has become a body of partisan politicians, rather than the moral arbiters of right versus wrong (spiritual justice). Of course, the Supreme Court should judge laws, not legislate laws. The system is sick and penicillin is not the cure.

Death and life are in the power of the tongue, not skin color (Proverbs 18:21). "For with the heart man believeth unto righteousness and with the mouth confession is made unto salvation" (Romans 10:10). This is precisely why individuals should not fear those individuals who desire to kill the body, civilians or policemen. "And fear not them which can kill the body, but are not able to kill the soul: but rather fear Him which is able to destroy both soul and body in hell" (Matthew 10:28). A word to the wise: "Don't get caught and die doing the devil's bidding."

The system is self-imploding because of the desire of the few for power, economic advantage and the economic greed factor. This overall state of affairs is fueled by the spiritual-moral ignorance of the many, and their desire for material things. In this kind of socio-economic climate, we have become a dog-eat-dog societal system (gun culture). Which, in turn, invariably will destroy us all, if we do not change to a more spiritual, loving, and serving attitude toward one another (just society) that is oriented toward mercy and grace. Christian friends, "We are troubled on every side, yet not distressed: we are perplexed, but not in despair; persecuted, but not forsaken, cast down, but not destroyed" (2 Corinthians 4:8-9). Furthermore, as Christians, we know, "He brought me up also out of a horrible pit, out of the miry clay, and set my feet upon a rock, and established my goings. And He hath put a new song in my mouth, even praise unto our God: many shall see it, and fear, and shall trust in the Lord" (Psalms 40:2-3). Selah!

24

THE TYRANNY OF THE MAJORITY

Most messengers are charismatic and famous, but the followers are the ones who create tyranny in a society. This is why social democracy requires an intelligent voting populace. Without a doubt, the Trump presidential campaign has an ungodly tyrannical mindset, because the battle cry "Make America Great Again" is about keeping America white privilege oriented. In fact, the slogan "Make America Great Again" is about the past, not the future. The future is about children. They are our future generations of Americans. And, everything in the past is under the precious blood of Jesus Christ, the Righteous One.

America's past belongs to the devil, because it was imperfect. Attempting to reclaim the past is a devilish enterprise. America's past was characterized by slavery, lynching, the KKK, institutional racism, Jim Crowism, the raping of women, and desegregation, not moral integration, racial profiling, and unfair criminal justice sentencing. We are in the present moment of the twenty first century, which in turn is characterized by cheap slave labor without chains: illegal immigration. Of course, this is why it exists.

The future belongs to God, so the question is: What will be America's response to the spiritual/moral challenges and demands? Ethnic chaos or national spiritual unity (One Nation Under God). Will it be more of the same ole same ole? Or can

America do the right thing?

In 1831, Alexis de Tocqueville accurately predicted the "Tyranny of the Majority in Modern Societies". How spiritually strange and socially frightening that an individual born over 210 years ago could envision a Donald Trump style personality becoming the standard bearer of a major political party. The Trump rise to power is like watching a horror movie. Tocqueville thought that American society was the spiritually and morally enlightened future of the world community, and that Europe was the glorious past. But, lo and behold, the Trump phenomenon and the reckless abandonment of the spiritual principles of the Preamble to the Constitution has happened.

In the twenty first century, the Christian Right has become the Christian wrong. The political party of freedom (Party of Abraham Lincoln) has become the Dixiecrat Party of the Southern Aristocracy: the "Good Ole Boy Corporate Network" (institutionalized corporate greed).

Behold the "spiritual mess" we find ourselves in: Men want to be women. Women want to be men. And, children do not know what to become, because no one desires spiritually to be what God created them to be. Genesis 1:27 states, "So God created man in his own image, in the image of God created he him; male and female created he them." The Christian church must accept the spiritual responsibility for the socio-economic-political confusion that exists in churches, as well as in American society. Make no mistake about it, the battle is the Lord's and the victory is already won: "For by grace are ye saved through faith; and that not of yourselves: it is the gift of God: not of works, lest any man should boast. For we are his workmanship, created in Christ

Jesus unto good works, which God hath before ordained that we should walk in them" (Ephesians 2: 8-10).

The Trump Presidency is simply about money. Nation-statehood is about spiritual values because the foundation of every society is family. This is why the U. S. Constitution does not glorify money. Money does not solve all problems. An individual cannot satisfy vanity because vanity is of the flesh. The Bible declares: "For the love of money is the root of all evil: which while some coveted after, they have erred from the faith, and pierced themselves through with many sorrows" (1 Timothy 6:10).

Every good, faithful, and decent Republican who is having a soul searching moment concerning the socio-political reality of Donald Trump as the "Grand Ole Party's Standard Bearer" is cringing because they know, "when he speaketh fair, believe him not: for there are seven abominations in his heart" (Proverbs 26: 25): The seven abominations are spiritually known as the seven deadly sins. Any individual that would publicly declare that they have nothing to ask God to forgive them for is dangerous. Self-righteousness is truly dangerous. Question: In the minds of some supporters is Trump the embodiment of the "second coming"?

In one way or another, every individual is spiritually oriented because of their moral-conscience. Just maybe the Republican Party can endure the public embarrassment of the Trump candidacy, and become more spiritually sensitive to the needs of all Americans, not just some Americans.

It is indeed troubling that America still has not found the spiritual formula for a just society, equity in economic resource allocation, liberty, and social justice for all American citizens.

The 2016 Presidential election has become a glaring negative example to the world community of what social democracy should never become. Social democracy is, and must always be, a positive example of equality, justice, and liberty for all, not exclusionary processes. Therefore, let's get out of the nation building business.

For after all, social democracy requires statesmen-like leadership, not political style manure. But, more importantly, democracy requires an intelligent, moral, and spiritual leadership-style mentality because a visionary leader must not have a yearning for the past, but a spiritual vision for the future (children). When all is said and done, a visionary leader knows how to help individuals become more spiritually, intellectually and morally healthy. At the same time, he/she can help individuals understand that they are interdependent upon each other instead of playing upon their lack of knowledge and spiritual understanding (the divide and conquer mentality).

"Let us therefore come boldly unto the throne of grace, that we may obtain mercy, and find grace to help in time of need" (Hebrews 4:16). Selah!

25
THE WELFARE SYSTEM

There are many legitimate reasons why some individuals must depend on a welfare system. Of course, individuals should not be dehumanized in order to become a recipient of welfare assistance. Both recipients, as well as welfare professionals, should be respectful of each other's human dignity (spirit). And, welfare assistance should not become a lifetime solution to what ought to be temporary problems. The underlying principle for receiving welfare assistance ought to be career development training coupled with daycare services, and of course, this process protects taxpayer resources by ultimately removing individuals from the welfare rolls.

We all know that church and state are entities that are constitutionally separate. However, there is another dimension that assists in developing the human spirit: "Beloved, I wish above all things that thou mayest prosper and be in health, even as thy soul prospereth" (3 John 1:2). Without a doubt, if welfare recipients just keep on living they will indeed discover this spiritual truism of life: "I have been young, and now am old; yet have I not seen the righteous forsaken, nor his seed begging bread" (Psalms 37:25). Therefore, in the receiving of welfare, above all things individuals should get a good understanding, because Welfare should not be a permanent way of life, but only a temporary means to a short-term end, because: "The Lord is my shepherd; and I shall not want" (Psalms 23:1).

Exampling a welfare lifestyle is not spiritually, mentally or physically healthy. But the worst kind of mental condition is to become materially wealthy, and not to have poured out your spirit in love and service to others. Mark 8:36 says, "For what shall it prosper a man, if he shall gain the whole world, and lose his own soul?"

Without a doubt, if welfare assistance is not managed appropriately, it can become spiritually and physically detrimental to an individual's mind, body, and soul. Trusting in a welfare system (human beings) rather than trusting in God can invariably become dangerous to an individual's psyche and spirit. Welfare recipients should not dehumanize themselves by seeking to maximize the pleasure principle, because "she that liveth in pleasure is dead while she liveth" (1 Timothy 5:6). But more importantly, choices have consequences. Bad choices, bad consequences. Good choices, good consequences. This is why welfare recipients should spiritually understand this Scripture: "Therefore take no thought, saying, What shall we eat? or, What shall we drink? or, Wherewithal shall we be clothed? (For after all these things do the Gentiles seek:) for your heavenly Father knoweth that ye have need of all these things. But seek ye first the kingdom of God, and his righteousness; and all these things shall be added unto you. Take therefore no thought for the morrow: for the morrow shall take thought for the things of itself. Sufficient unto the day is the evil thereof" (Matthew 6:31-34).

The welfare system was primarily created as a hedge against abject poverty for whites, but the negative image of welfare was projected upon minorities, especially blacks. The socio-economic system was designed to perpetuate white family economic success. When white families fail, they invariably blame minorities rather than themselves. The welfare system allows dysfunctional white families to project and scapegoats their lack of economic success on permanent-tan minorities, especially blacks. Of course, minorities project their lack of family socio-economic success upon the system (whites). Both approaches have some truth associated with them. However, one side has more truth associated with it than the other side because one side established all the rules and then changed the rules to fit their socio-political-economic objectives.

It seems as though allowing blacks to benefit from welfare is more beneficial to the socio-political-economic purposes of the system than allowing blacks to have gainfully meaningful employment opportunities. Above all, welfare destroys the God-given image of family structure. Government becomes the head of the household, and at the same time determines who goes and who stays in the house. Of course, the welfare system would be more humane and spiritually right in the sight of God if it allowed for men to remain in the household as long as they are gainfully employed. Men must have job because a job is a job and any job is better than no job. Picking up trash is a job. Flipping hamburgers is a job. Work is God's gift to men, and all work is honorable in the sight of God because a servant is worth his hire.

Therefore, a welfare system based upon the proportional income of the head of the household is a spiritually family-friendly societal approach to the problem of family poverty. American society should never condone "shacking up", that is, men and women living together without being legally married, because a spiritually oriented society begins in the nuclear family unit. God is a God of obligation and in shacking up there is no obligation.

Both welfare recipients, as well as all Americans should align themselves with the Word of God in order to become overcomers of immoral societal confusion (policies). We all should know that there is a spiritual struggle within, and at the same time, we know that: "The wages of sin is death, but the gift of God is eternal life through Jesus Christ our Lord" (Romans 6:23). All of us should desire to become what God desires, that we become through Him like Jesus by loving and serving each other in his name. America, take heed of this Scriptural reference: "The Spirit of the Lord is upon me, because he hath anointed me to preach the gospel to the poor: he hath sent me to heal the brokenhearted, to preach deliverance to the captives, and recovering of sight to the blind, to set at liberty them that are bruised, to preach the acceptable year of the Lord" (The Great Commission; Luke 4: 18-19). Selah!

26
UNQUALIFIED

The spiritual definition of leadership is the visionary ability of an individual to take others where they have not been spiritually and morally and to do so in love and service in Jesus's name. This, in and of itself, is a monumental spiritual undertaking. After all, social democracy requires a team-building leadership mentality and there is no "I" in the concept team. Unfortunately, too many so-called leaders are victimized by the personal-pronoun disease. And, partisan politics cannot alter this divisive reality. A team building social democracy approach lends itself to positive compromise.

There is the past moment, present moment, and future moment. Everything in the past is under the blood of Jesus Christ "for we must all appear before the judgment seat of Christ: that every one may receive the things done in his body, according to that he hath done, whether it be good or bad" (2 Corinthians 5:10). We live and have our being in the present moment. And, it is the "now-ness" of it all that we must share with one with another. Without a doubt, the future belongs to God. "All that the Father giveth me shall come to me; and him that cometh to me I will in no wise cast out" (John 5:37). There is no future in casting out, because casting out represents death.

Therefore, we can only learn from the past because we live and have our being in the now, and have eternal hope for the future (our children). Indeed, our children are our future, as well as, a heritage from God. We have been taught and spiritually understand that "...all things work together for good to them that love God, to them who are called according to his purpose" (Romans 8:28). All Americans should stand up and hold fast to the basic spiritual tenets of our social democracy because we know that there is a higher reality to our very existence. "What? Know ye not that your body is the temple of the Holy Ghost which is in you, which ye have of God, and ye are not your own?" (1 Corinthians 6:19). Hence, denying any immigrant the opportunity to come to America based upon religious doctrine is to deny the righteousness of God and one's own self.

Non-spiritual-minded leaders can always concoct a Kool-Aid-Drink, and ask the American public to drink of this, and it will set them free. And, of course, some individuals will be tempted to drink, and others will drink the Kool-Aid. There will always be some individuals who will desire power, money, political influence, and privilege for the few, but not for all. Thank God, America was founded by the people, of the people, and for the people. Get ready people, the train is coming, get on board with three fruits of the Spirit and sound spiritual and political doctrine: Love, joy, and peace. We are a democratic country of immigrants of all nationalities, and "What shall we then say to these things? If God be for us, who can be against us?" (Romans 8:31). Jesus said, "Go ye into all the world, and preach the Gospel to every creature. He that believeth and is baptized shall be saved: but he that believeth not shall be damned" (Mark 15:15-16). As Americans we should be embracing the Great Commission of Jesus, and speaking boldly what is inscribed on the Statute of Liberty. All Christians know and understand "Nevertheless the foundation of God standeth sure, having this seal. The Lord knoweth them that are his. And, Let every one that nameth the name of Christ depart from iniquity" (2 Timothy 2:19). Christ is a spiritual title that means righteousness.

America is on the brink of political leadership disaster. We are caught in a political disastrous quagmire that will invariably bring America to her knees. Money is not God, and the negative use of power is not of God. Negative leadership mentalities diminish the moral fabric of a nation. For, every God-fearing individual knows that "Righteousness exalteth a nation: but sin is a reproach to any people" (Proverbs 14:34).

All Americans need to pray for righteous leadership so we can embrace a culturally inclusive America because out of one blood, God created all nations. Leadership should set the example that we as American citizens can talk and walk in it. "For even hereunto were ye called: because Christ also suffered for us, leaving us an example, that ye should follow his steps" (1 Peter 2:21). Therefore, a leader knows that he should "Let this mind be in you, which was also in Christ Jesus" (Philippians 2:5). A leader, who thinks before speaking understands the new commandment of Jesus, "A new commandment I give unto you, That ye love one another" (John 13:34). Good leadership is not about saying what one thinks, but what one knows in God. Romans 15:5-7 states, "Now the God of patience and consolation grant you to be likeminded one toward another according to Christ Jesus: That ye may with one mind and one mouth glorify God, even the father of our Lord Jesus Christ. Wherefore receive ye one another, as Christ also received us, to the glory of God".

The following are some positive principles regarding having a leadership mentality:

- A spiritual leader thinks before speaking. "For as he

thinketh in his heart, so is he" (Proverbs 23:7). "A good name is rather to be chosen than great riches, and loving favor rather than silver and gold" (Proverbs 22:1).

- A good leader stresses the positive rather than the negative, because it is just as easy, but being positive is godlike, and being negative is devilish. A good leader even when he deals with the negative deals with it in a positive manner.

In conclusion, the American people deserve a leadership mentality that brings forth the best in us, not the worst. It has been proven that our democratic system of governance is the best despite its flaws. Fellow Americans, "Let your moderation be known unto all men. The Lord is at hand. Be careful for nothing: but in everything by prayer and supplication with thanksgiving let your requests be made known unto God. And the peace of God, which passeth all understanding, shall keep your hearts and minds through Christ Jesus" (Philippians 4:5-7).

27

AMERICAN SOCIETY: UPSIDE-DOWN AND UNDER-WATER

The election of Donald J. Trump to the Office of President spiritually and morally flipped American society upside down. Perceived notions of White Privilege(s) that was at the core of the Trumpster's election is something for nothing. Of course, this attitude is not new to American society. It has always been beneath the surface, above the surface, in the air, and everywhere in White consciousness. As a result, the election of Donald J. Trump to the sacred Office of President of these United States of America is simply an ungodly, non-spiritual, and immoral depiction of who we truly are as a people.

America fought a Civil War to become united. Prayerfully and hopefully, we will not have to fight another Civil War in order to remain united as "one nation under God with liberty and justice for all." The appointments of Stephen K. Bannon, a well-known White Nationalist, as Chief White House Advisor and Senator Jefferson Sessions as the Chief Law Enforcement Officer (Attorney General) are, to say the least, disconcerting, bothersome, and extremely troublesome. I use the nomenclature "Trumpster" because the writer, as well as all Americans, should respect the Office of the President. And the Trumpster has not been sworn in as the 45th President. This is why it is appropriate to refer to an individual as he presents himself to the public (a hook and a crook). Without a doubt, individuals cannot make that which is unclean clean (Job 14:4).

Many Americans have emphatically pronounced, "Let's give him a chance." A chance to do what? The Trumpster has already shown his true colors: White and White privilege only! We are upside down because "righteousness exalteth a nation: but sin is a reproach to any people" (Proverbs 14:34). To be sure, White supremacy does not exalt a multicultural nation; it only denigrates American society. Again, the appointment of Stephen K. Bannon is an enigma in the middle of a riddle because Donald J. Trump was elected to the Presidency by debasing the multicultural nature of American society. The minorities who, for thirty pieces of silver (and this represents only a spiritually symbolic amount a.k.a. Judas revenue), must be carefully watched, observed, and above all, prayed for, because they have already given their souls and minds to an ungodly personality.

Why are we underwater? "Underwater" is primarily real estate terminology, but the concept clearly expresses the nature of an immoral society. Electing a Presidential leader that does not understand the ethical consequences of words is truly frightening to the nth degree. Words matter. This is precisely why the Bible emphatically states, "Keep thy tongue from evil, and thy lips from speaking guile. Depart from evil, and do good; seek peace, and pursue it" (Psalms 34:13-14). By the way, "Death and life are in the power of the tongue: and they that love it shall eat the fruit thereof" (Proverbs 18:21). Words matter. If they didn't, why read the Holy Bible? All individuals must clearly understand that "in the beginning was the Word, and the Word was with God, and the Word was God" (John 1:1).

The words coming from the mouth of the President-elect during the campaign were not words of endearment, encouragement, or national unity. Words have consequences because words can lead to positive as well as negative actions. During the campaign, we did not hear Donald J. Trump utter any spiritual words of meditation, only words of hatred and division in his speeches. "Let the words of my mouth, and the meditation of my heart, be acceptable in thy sight, O Lord, my strength, and redeemer" (Psalms 19:14). Or these profound words: "let your speech be always with grace, seasoned with salt, that ye may know how ye ought to answer every man" (Colossians 4:6). President-elect Donald J. Trump spoke ungodly divisive words that can only appeal to the worst instincts of humankind, even physically mocking disabled individuals. Without a doubt, Secretary Clinton only needed to recite the words that came from the mouth of Donald J. Trump; no more or no less. The Trumpster's own words convict him. Therefore, let's not naively misunderstand the undercurrent that was propelling the election of the Trumpster to the Office of the Presidency. It was not loss of jobs, political gridlock, or trade agreements, but the tanning/multicultural nature of American society and the perceived loss of White privilege(s).

President-elect Donald J. Trump, give your loyal voters/ supporters what they voted for and what you have faithfully promised: Build the wall, tall and wide; ban immigrants based-upon religion, especially Muslims; profile minorities; repeal the Affordable Healthcare Act (Obamacare); keep on denying that climate change is not man-made; and make an ungodly political alliance with Putin. However, in the final analysis, we all know that God has the last word simply because "the earth is the Lord's, and the fullness thereof; the world, and they that dwell therein" (Psalms 24:1). But, more importantly, "Thou art worthy, O Lord, to receive glory and honour and power: for thou hast created all things, and for thy pleasure they are and were created"

(Revelations 4:11). America, you can believe these scriptures and have life, and life more abundantly. Or you can believe in a "hook" called Santa Claus.

America, God is a just God, and He sometimes gives us what we want, not what we need. A lot of Americans voted for Donald J. Trump as President, and he is the President-elect. In the past, America was strong (spiritually, morally, and militarily), but we walked softly and carried a big stick. By the way, America still is the strongest nation, militarily and economically, on earth by any standard of measurement. President Obama has talked the talk and walked the walk, in a highly sophisticated diplomatic Presidential behavioral attitude against selfish oppositional odds (Republicans).

Ultimately, every human being is a graveyard traveller, but individuals should not have a graveyard mentality or a ditch digging mentality. This is precisely why Jesus condensed the Ten Commandments to the Two Great Commandments: "Thou shalt love the Lord thy God with all thy heart, and with all thy soul, and with all thy mind. This is the first and great commandment. And the second is like unto it. Thou shalt love thy neighbor as thyself. On these two commandments hang all the law and prophets" (Matthew 22: 37-39). Selah!

28

WHAT IN THE "HELL" DO YOU HAVE TO LOSE?

In a recent so-called policy speech in front of a 99.9 percent White audience in the State of Michigan, Donald Trump, the standard bearer, for the Grand Ole Party (Republican Party), asked this political policy question of the Black community: "What in the Hell do you have to lose"? Black America; let's be perfectly clear about what we have to lose. Of course, Mr. Trump gave no policy specifics of how this great socio-economic transformation would take place. "Just TRUST me." Native Americans trusted: Behold the results. In the Black American experience, the Ronald Reagan doctrine is most germane to the potential Presidency of a Donald Trump: "When he speaketh fair, believe him not: for there are seven abominations in his heart: (The seven deadly sins)" (Proverbs 26:25).

In analyzing the so-called policy speech further, Mr. Trump, apologized in general for off-the-cuff comments in the heat of battle; apologizing to no one specifically, because it would take three months, and his pursuit of the presidency would be over. For example, Trump called Jeb Bush "low energy," President Obama is not an American citizen, Ted Cruz's father had something to do with the assassination of President Kennedy, Mexicans are thieves, rapists, and robbers, displayed contempt for a Gold Star Family, insulted Senator John McCain, and above all, keep immigrants from entering the country based upon religion. These are only a few examples of utter disrespect and disregard for American citizens, and the list goes on, on, and on. And, at the same time, Mr. Trump has high regards for a foreign leader (Putin) whose policies are oriented toward dictatorship, spying, lying, cyber warfare, weakening America's influence in NATO, and above all, taking over other countries through militarism (barrel of guns). This, in and of, itself is a complete disrespect of America and her democratic principles and policies.

In case you do not know it, allow this scripture to tell you so: Every way of a man is right in his own eyes: but the Lord pondereth the hearts (Proverbs 21:2). Without a doubt, in the final analysis: There is a way which seemeth right unto a man, but the end thereof are the ways of death (Proverbs 14: 12).

Black America, Donald Trump, said vote for him, because" what in the hell do you have to lose" if you give your sacred vote to him. This is what you have to lose: the 1964 Civil Rights Act and the 1965 Voting Rights Act. Enumerated below are the most important things you will lose, because there are some things that money cannot buy:

- Intellectual integrity and moral character: Take heed, and beware of covetousness: for a man's life consisteth not in the abundance of the things which he possesseth (Luke 12:15). All individuals, some glad morning, including Donald Trump will be confronted with this judgment reality: For what shall it profit a man; if he shall gain the whole world, and lose his own soul? (Luke 8: 36).
- Promises made by a man such as a Donald Trump mean absolutely nothing, but promises made by God mean everything, because God is a promise keeper, not a promise breaker. Nor is God a heartbreaker. Behold God's promise:

Whereby is given unto us exceeding great and precious promises: that by these ye might be partakers of the divine nature, having escaped the corruption that is in the world through lust (2 Peter 1:4). And, lust is one of the seven deadly sins.

- Speaking ill of any ethnic/racial or religious group of individuals in a democracy that is built by immigrants is an affront to all Americans, because all of us should understand: Nevertheless the foundation of God standeth sure, having this seal. The Lord knoweth them that are his. And, let everyone that nameth the name of Christ depart from iniquity (2 Timothy 2:19). Mr. Trump, please know full well that God can handle his business. Show us your taxes in order that Americans might understand that you can handle your personal business. And, of course, your leadership idol Russian Dictator Putin will know as well.

- A man is known by the company he keeps; especially loyal supporters. Therefore, Be not deceived: evil communications corrupt good manners (1 Corinthians 14:33). Hanging out with individuals who seek to promulgate White Privilege policies and processes, glorify bigotry, and build exclusionary walls is a special kind of mindset. There is a time-honored socio-psychological slogan that goes like this: Association brings about assimilation. In fact, the Bible speaks emphatically concerning these types of personalities (authoritarianism): Answer not a fool according to his folly, lest thou also be like unto him. Answer not a fool according to his folly, lest he be wise in his own conceit (Proverbs 26: 45).

- It is a documented social fact of public life that the thought processes of Donald Trump leave an awful lot to be desired: For as he thinketh in his heart, so is he (Proverbs 23:7).

Black America the sacred right to vote was denied as a birthright of American citizenship, because of skin color. Voting rights were earned by the shedding of blood and death. Of course, many Whites died helping in the cause of the sacred right to vote, .e.g., The Three Civil Rights Workers in Mississippi (Schwerner, Goodman, and Chaney). And, of course, there were many other Whites who lost their lives as well in the Voting Rights Struggle. Without a doubt, voting for Donald Trump as the presidential leadership image of America would give national sanction to religious bigotry, racism, sexism, and in general a national display of malnutrition of the brain to the nth degree. Black supporters of Donald Trump beware, because all money is not good money: For the love of money is the root of all evil: which while some coveted after, they have erred from the faith, and pierced themselves through with many sorrows (1 Timothy 6:10). A word to the wise is sufficient: Black supporters of Donald Trump be prayerful. The Republican Party since 1964 (Senator Barry Goldwater) has been shredding the principles of the Party of Lincoln (Grand Ole Party: National Unity), and now the Republican Party is the old Dixiecrat Party of the Southern Confederacy. Donald Trump has proven, beyond the shadow of a doubt, that the Confederacy is alive and doing well in all of America, because Silence is Consent. Selah!

29
WHAT'S GOING ON?

In the twentieth century, an infamous flawed singer, Marvin Gaye, asked the question, "What going on?" This question is still relevant today in twenty-first century America, because we are moving from one confused moral state of existence to a higher level of moral confusion; there seems to be no end in sight. This is why we must become spiritually intelligent enough to understand the solution (answer) to the question, because whatever is going on is not good for American society.

Subsequently, we are more segregated and politically divided today than we were prior to the passage of the 1964 Civil Rights Act and the 1965 Voting Rights Act (Jim Crow Era). The question is why: what's going on? In part the answers lie in these socio-economic-political-religious realities:

- The breakdown of the nuclear family structure. Too many children being born out of wedlock is a serious spiritual, moral, and societal problem that must be remedied. Children must be taught character development traits and spiritual values at home, before going to church and school. Tough love must be shown in the home environment. Children must be given positive modeling behavior responsibilities in their home environments.
- Educational institutions are allowing too much of the societal "instant-gratification" confusion to influence the structure of schooling; which in turn, influences educational development (thought processes). This has

produced the: me, myself, and I syndrome. The human mind is our greatest resource, and not enough economic capital goes into the development of minds and hearts (attitudes). We need a better quality of professional teaching in our educational institutions, and teachers who have the spiritual desire and professional ability to motivate, develop, and inspire the students entrusted in their care.

- The current two-party-political system has divided America by race/ethnicity, social class, religion, and gender discrimination. Even so much so that some seek to keep "certain" individuals from exercising their Constitutional sacred right to vote. Lest we forget, charity begins at home, and then spreads abroad. This in and of itself creates political governing confusion-polarization. But, more importantly, the "corporate party" that is big money (dark money) is controlling public policy by buying elections and influencing voting patterns.

- One of the primary obstacles to societal unity is workplace economic-discrimination. Most Americans know that work is a spiritual commandment from God (the gift of God): no work, no eat (Genesis 3:19). Work is a spiritual obligatory reality with a sacred purpose.

- Eliminate gender discrimination in the workplace and social structure of society: equal pay for equal work.

- We need a "dollar" that circulates at least three times in underdeveloped and underserved communities as common-sense-spiritual solutions for economic justice. Governmental incentives should be given to entrepreneurial investors who are willing to provide goods and services in economically deprived communities (income inequality issues).

- Law enforcement agencies must be transparent in their

policies, procedures, and enforcement of violations of laws. No ethnic-category, social class or religious persuasion of individuals should be profiled by police departments.

State legislatures should enact laws mandating civilian review boards with subpoena power in order to ensure police-citizen-accountability. Police officers are the first line of defense for apprehending law-breakers, and they should never become the judge, jury and executioner.

Police departments should be very, very concerned about "stand your ground" laws, and the open carry of firearms. These types of laws make community policing more difficult and potentially more unsafe. Body cameras have become a social justice must both for the legal protection and civil rights of citizens as well as policemen.

Police officers must be professionally trained in techniques of how to handle family domestic disputes and violence emergency calls.

Police car-chasing incidents have become life and death situations both for policemen as well as civilians, and therefore helicopter and drone-surveillance should be the first-line of defense used in pursuit of criminals. Community-neighborhood policing is needed in order to foster better community and police relations (societal stability and social justice). In addition, policemen (citizen policemen) should be given financial incentives to live in the communities-neighborhoods in which they serve. This will help reduce the fear-factor associated with policing in urban environments.

Sunday morning at eleven o'clock is still the most segregated hour in American society. Question: why? (Individuals of the same religious persuasion, serving the same invisible God, but cannot worship that spiritual God together in the same physical buildings: choice). This is a monumental spiritual problem. Most of all, churches should model "charity: love and service". Christian churches are speaking "social-truths", but not the kinds of spiritual truths that make individuals free (John 8: 31-32).

In conclusion, "For the leaders of this people cause them to err; and they that are led of them are destroyed. Therefore the Lord shall have no joy in their young men, neither shall have mercy on their fatherless and widows: for every one is a hypocrite and an evildoer, and every mouth speaketh folly. For all this his anger is not turned away, but his hand is stretched out still" (Isaiah 9:16-17). "For all have sinned, and come short of the glory of God" (Romans 3:23). At one time, we were in some superficial symbolic respects "one nation under God". Today, America has become a "No-God" society, because too many Americans do not want to spiritually know God. Selah!

30
WHOM DO YOU LOVE MORE: CREATOR OR CREATION?

The Trump Presidential Candidacy is about loving the creation more than the Creator, and above all, loving himself more so than Americans of every skin color. "Thou art worthy, O Lord, to receive glory and honor and power: for thou hast created all things, and for thy pleasure do they are and were created" (Revelation 4:11). Make no mistake about it: Donald Trump is one of God's creation, not the Creator. First of all, let's be perfectly clear about this spiritual truism. Every individual regardless of cultural origin is God's creation. No individual created himself or herself! And, God does not make mistakes. Only human beings make mistakes, and then try to rationalize "away" their mistakes.

When Donald Trump tells you who he is, what he believes, why he believes it, and what he will do if given the opportunity to do so, why not accept him for his own words. Life and death are in the tongue. Trump is simply an individual who is hell-bent on hooking and crooking for material things. "For as he thinketh in his heart, so is he: Eat and drink, saith he to thee; but his heart is not with thee" (Proverbs 23:7). Simply put, Trump's philosophy about life is: "use other people's money" And we can add not pay his fair share of income taxes. This is precisely why Trump will not publicly disclose his taxes, because it will reveal that he has hood-winked the tax system, that is, not paid his fair share of federal income taxes. But, more importantly, his taxes will reveal what foreign investors and communistic-minded dictators" he is in bed with. To be sure, strange politics make for strange bedfellows. For believers in the Trump doctrine of (ethnic bigotry, sexism, racism, and religious bigotry) ask yourselves this spiritual question: "Can two walk together, except they be agreed" (Amos 3:3). We, all should know: "Jesus Christ the same yesterday, and today, and forever" (Hebrews 13:8). Someone from the Christian Right Evangelical Movement who is not a lover of "material-things", please inform the Donald that life is more than just money; even if it is other people's money: "Take heed, and beware of covetousness: for a man's life consisteth not in the abundance of things which he possesseth" (Luke 12:15).

Donald Trump wants the American people to believe in him, trust that he can do what he says he can do, and above all, accept him as an international successful businessman that knows how to create jobs. My fellow Americans, an individual should never be given a job"simply because he desires the job. But, give an individual a job, because he is in fact intellectually capable of doing the job (and functions and tasks associated with the job).

Here's what all Americans already know or should know about social democracy as a governmental system. American social democracy is based primarily upon spiritual values, not just material values. God has already given us dominion over the world in the four-fold foundation decree: "And God blessed them, and God said unto them, Be fruitful, and multiply, and replenish the earth, and subdue it, and have dominion over the fish of the sea, and over the fowl of the air, and over every living thing that moveth upon the earth" (Genesis 1:28). And, we can add, "except a woman." We are in this together, because women just like men have free-will and they are responsible for their own soul's salvation.

If an individual such as Donald Trump can be elected to the highest office in the world-community the Presidency of the United States of America; then God help us all, males and females. We all know: "For what shall it profit a man, if he shall gain the whole world, and lose his own soul?" (Mark 8: 36). Therefore, if the Donald Trump Mentality is elected President of these United States of America, America loses, and the world loses, as well. It is, indeed, unfortunate that apparently Donald Trump had a call to deliver America from itself. The call either came from the light side or the dark side; however, judging from his rhetoric unmistakably it appears as though it is from the dark side.

Read the preamble to the U.S Constitution, as well as, the Constitution and you will be spiritually enlightened. In fact, the founders of our socio-economic-political-system knew that all Americans should be able to read. Therefore, a universal mass educational system was instituted in order that all individuals learn to read; especially read the Bible, because reading the Bible helps individuals to understand the spiritual meaning of God acting to redeem human history. Therefore, even God has said: "Blessed is he that readeth..." (Revelation 1:3). The Preamble to the U.S. Constitution, as well as, the U. S. Constitution itself is Bible-based, but in a different form and format. Of course, the Framers had good intentions, but they were also "hypocrites", because their words and actions were not congruent. Reading is spiritually developmental, as well as, socially enlightening. And, of course, this is the reason why social democracy only takes root in certain types of societies and not others.

The spiritual purpose of religion is to unify individuals; not divide individuals from the truth of God, that equal is equal, not that equal is more or less equal. God chooses leaders that he knows by name, and have found grace in his sight. Moses was such a leader, not comparing in any way Moses and Trump, but we must ask the question: Is the Donald such a man as was Moses? "And the Lord said unto Moses, I will do this thing also that thou hast spoken: for thou hast found grace in my sight, and I know thee by name" (Exodus 33:17). Without a doubt, material success will test both your moral, as well as, mental-intellectual-character. Death is the socio-spiritual equalizer, because regardless of ethnicity, sex-status, or skin color death is certain. "And as it is appointed unto men once to die, but after this the judgment: so Christ was once offered to bear the sins of many; and unto them that look for him shall he appear the second time without sin unto salvation" (Hebrews 9:27-28).

God is the only spiritually-unifying-force in the universe. The devil is a spiritual-trickster and a confusion instigator. America, God is spiritually watching and waiting in 2016. Question: Can we spiritually get back home to God, before it is too late, because the Trumpster should not make America lose her spiritual blessings as the nation-state (LIGHT) set on a hill illuminating "points of light" around the world. Selah!

31

WHY BLACKS AND WHITES DO NOT WORSHIP TOGETHER

There is only one God and He is the only one that has the right to play God because He is God. God is Spirit and they that worship him must worship him in Spirit and Truth. Whites are not God. Blacks are not God. Skin color is definitely not God regardless of the color. God is God all by himself because He is the source of all things. Without a doubt, physical death is the social equalizer in the equation between Whites and Blacks as well as males and females. Spiritual death is altogether another issue.

Question: Why don't Blacks and Whites worship together? In my opinion, there are two overriding primary reasons: (A) White institutionalization of the notion of white superiority and, (B) different worship styles based upon distinct cultural traditions. When we cannot tell the truth to ourselves we obviously cannot tell the truth to others. Herein lies the crux of the spiritual problem that is individuals not absolutely being honest with each other. Whites lie to other Whites. Blacks lie to other Blacks. As results, some individuals seeking to control the truth cause us to end-up in a state of confusion. "For God is not the author of confusion, but of peace, as in all churches of the saints" (1 Corinthians 14:33).

White pastors generally teach self-reliance and self-discipline through God. Black pastors emotionally preach that God will do everything and no self-discipline or self-initiatives are required.

Free-will makes God not a divine Santa Claus. Prayer without works is dead. White pastors in general take the guilty stain off parishioners and Black pastors place the guilty stain on parishioners. That is, Black pastors preach what they understand to be the most important thing about living and the spiritual rite of passage: salvation and being born again.

Experiential lifestyles and family resource differences causes the content of sermons and delivery styles in Black and White churches to be vastly different. These facts also account for different motives for worship and church attendance. Without a doubt, both White and Black pastors play very loose and free with the Word of God.

Church attendance in the White community is about perpetuating cultural Whiteness (societal and family traditions). Church attendance in the Black community is about perpetuating cultural Blackness based upon the dehumanization of Blackness. God and godly living is left out of the worship equation. Worshipping God ought to be about individuals understanding godly principles and spirituality, not racial and cultural glorification. Praising God is for glorification of the goodness of God. God is good all the time and He is greatly to be praised. To be sure, "God judgeth the righteous, and God is angry with the wicked every day" (Psalm 7:11).

Church attendance in both Black and White communities must be transformed into love and service concerning a Living God, who redeems humanity, cares for humanity and above all forgives us of ours sins. When this takes place both Blacks and Whites can praise God from whom all blessings flow together in love, peace and joy. Then and only then will worship become our faithful service and godly love for each other.

Values and social barriers that are deep-rooted in cultural differences and family traditions are very difficult to break down and of course some of them are good, but they are not God. A lot of what goes on in both Black and Whites churches have absolutely nothing to do with God. In fact, in many twenty-first century churches there is no reverence for God. This is why Blacks and Whites can party together on Saturday night but cannot worship God together on Sunday morning. We can socialize together but not spiritualize together. Apparently, we are not serving the same God. On Sundays we shop in shopping malls together. Why can't we worship God together in Christian churches?

On the one hand, Whites have been free all of their lives and indeed American society was established for Whites to experience individual and family related success. While, on the other hand, America was designed for Blacks to serve Whites. Unfortunately, some Whites attitudinally still feel that the American social system gives them superiority over Blacks. Case in point, the vulgar disrespect displayed by some Whites toward the Office of the President simply because a Black man is the president. Whatever happened to the "principle" of respect for the position; even if you have disdain for the individual who holds the position?

In twenty-first century America far too many Americans do not want to follow the principles of God in the Bible for spiritual salvation. In many cases we are not worshipping God in the Spirit, but men in the flesh. In fact, in some situations church attendance has simply become a best-dressed contest, not an occasion for holiness. There is nothing wrong with giving God your best; even in dress.

Sin is a spiritual problem. Institutional racism is a spiritual problem that creates a sin-hatred -chasm. Racism has oriented life in American society toward skin-color rather than God, godly living and spiritual understanding. Therefore, hatred is the primary reason why Blacks and Whites cannot worship together. As a result, the objective on both sides of the isle is to perpetuate racial cultural distinctiveness, rather than God-centered Christianity and godly living. But we all know that all of us are God's children.

In the conclusion of the matter God hates racism. Hatred creates separation from God and above all societal confusion. There is no hatred in heaven and therefore no need for a Civil Rights Movement. Having peace as in all of the churches of the saints will invariably stop our insatiable desire to prostitute the church of Jesus Christ for personal gain reasons, rather glorifying God the Creator of all things including skin-color. "The rich and the poor meet together: the Lord is the maker of them all." And, of course, in the end, both die. Question: why can't we worship together? (Proverbs: 22:2). Selah.

32
AMERICA'S NATIONAL SECURITY DISASTER

When you are a voice crying in the wilderness of spiritual ignorance of God's principles, precepts, concepts, anything that can happen, will (did) happen, and the happening can literally destroy a democratic nation. "The fear of the Lord is the instruction of wisdom; and before honour is humility" (Proverbs 15:33). Every American must pray, and at the same time, spiritually understand what to pray for: Peace on earth and good will toward all. Pray, pray, and pray, because "Righteousness exalteth a nation: but sin is a reproach to any people" (Proverbs 14:34). It is, indeed, midnight in America, and not morning as former President Reagan declared.

With the election of Donald J. Trump to the Office of President, did America's national interests and security become the "Art Of The Deal"? America's national interests must be spiritually grounded in human rights (individual freedom), diplomacy, national security interests of the nation, and to prevent the loss of human life through wars. National security is not simply securing and protecting the economic interests of the rich and powerful. Our diplomatic core of professionals should spiritually understand, above all else, "Lay hands suddenly on no man, neither be partaker of other men's sins: keep thyself pure" (1 Timothy 5:22). The Trump Administration needs to clearly understand this verse, because hatred is evil and can become a killer. The first obligation of any presidential administration is to keep the country safe, because you cannot make the country great unless it is first safe.

Power corrupts, and absolute power corrupts absolutely. Therefore, "Let all things be done decently and in order" (1 Corinthians 14: 40). Worldly (human) power concedes nothing, but takes everything. While, on the other hand, God's spiritual power declares, "And we know that all things work together for good to them that love God, to them who are the called according to his purpose" (Romans 8:28).

Blacks, who are meeting with President-elect Trump, need to clearly understand that an individual should never meet with a person of the moral character of President-elect Trump alone; take a witness. Trust, but verify is the primary role of a witness regarding what was said by whom. However, given the despicable things the Trumpster has said about minorities, why converse with such a double-minded individual? Would you attempt to have a conversation with Lucifer? Lucifer is too slick for any God-fearing mortal individual to attempt to hold a conversation with him. The devil is absolutely too cunning, Not by any stretch of the imagination is Donald J. Trump the devil. However, the Trumpster's language, style, demeaning conversations concerning women and minorities, dismissal of an entire religion as grounded in terrorism, and bold-faced lies convict him as a servant of the devil's will. God-fearing individuals should never have a conversation with the devil, because he is too slick. Graveyard travelling mortals must always rely on the intercessor, JESUS. Even Jesus said these words to the devil, and He was the Son of God, "It is written again, Thou shalt not tempt the Lord thy God" (Matthew 4:7). Because, "No one can serve two masters: for either he will hate the one, and love the other; or else he will hold to the one, and despise the other. Ye cannot serve God and mammon" (Matthew 6:24). According to the language of President-elect Trump, we know full well he will serve mammon (money). This is precisely why we have not seen his personal income taxes, and Republicans will not insist that he reveal them. Moreover, his cabinet selections are vivid indicators of who will be served, and to be sure, it is not the American people. In fact, the only reason why President-elect Trump admires Putin is because he is slicker and a bigger lover of himself. As a matter of fact, this is why during the political campaign he stated that he admired and respected Putin rather than America's democratically elected President Barack Obama.

Leadership is about relationships, and relationships can be spiritually healthy or spiritually unhealthy. For example, former 2012 Republican Presidential Candidate Mitt Romney in a public speech boldly told the unadulterated truth about President-elect Trump prior to November 8th. On the other hand, when the Trumpster said that Mitt Romney wanted his support so badly in 2012 that he was willing to drop to his knees, we didn't know whether the Trumpster was telling the truth or a bold-face lie. Now, we all know! Donald J. Trump is a Master Entertainer who cunningly knows how to appeal to the emotions of individuals, and above all, entice them to think based upon their emotions, prejudices, and fears. And, this is precisely why Donald J. Trump was elected President, and America is upside-down, and topsy-turvy.

When an individual publicly declares that he has nothing for which he needs to ask God to forgive him for, and of course, such a declaration implies that he is without sin. However, King David, whom God declared was a man after his own heart, emphatically stated the opposite of the Trumpster's declaration: "For I acknowledge my transgressions: and my sin is ever before me" (Psalms 51:3). Furthermore, David said: "Behold, I was shapen in iniquity, and in sin did my mother conceive me" (Psalms 51:5). Moreover, King David understood that sin was lawlessness, because all sin is unrighteousness. This is why Jesus said to the men who brought the woman, who was found in adultery, but not the man: "He that is without sin among you, let him first cast a stone at her" (John 8:7). More importantly, "If we say that we have no sin, we deceive ourselves, and the truth is not in us" (1 John 1:8). While, on the other hand, The Gospel Writer Paul declares: "For all have sinned, and come short of the glory of God" (Romans 3:23).

In closing, the Electoral College "must" certify the election results, because Trump's White Nationalist supporters will destroy American society if he is not. Trump lied, Russian cyber-hackers helped him (Putin), he degraded minorities, women, the Islamic religion, and more importantly, did not receive the majority of the popular vote. But, America, don't worry, because in the final analysis Trump will be impeached, because he will be caught attempting to make America the art of the deal, not GREAT. Selah!

33

WORDS AND ELECTIONS HAVE CONSEQUENCES

Words matter and have consequences, because "Death and life are in the power of the tongue: and they that love it shall eat the fruit thereof" (Proverbs 18:21). Elections matter and have consequences. "For as he thinketh in his heart, so is he: Eat and drink, saith he to thee; but his heart is not with thee" (Proverbs 23:7). What President-elect Trump has boldly and sinfully stated concerning many Americans; therefore, as Americans, it should be extremely difficult for any spiritually and morally-minded American to respect the man. But, as Americans, we must respect the Office of the Presidency. Convince an immoral man against his own will, you leave him immoral, still.

The 2016 Presidential election ushered in an ungodly war unlike any in America's torrid history, because it is strictly spiritual and mental warfare, not physical. The election of Donald J. Trump to the office of president poses a real spiritual-moral dilemma for the American people as well as America's Constitutional governing document. The Power of the Office rests with the American people. But, the privilege to love and serve is given to the individual who is blessed to be elected to the Office of the Presidency. President-elect Donald J. Trump is attempting to flip the script. To date, thus far, he has been fairly successful in doing so. Words and elections have both material as well as spiritual consequences.

Questions: Is America First? Is the Trump family first and last? Or is Russia's national interest 1.1 times greater than America's national interests? It seems as though President-elect Trump is playing foot-loose and fancy-free with America's national interests and national security. Moreover, American lives are caught in the middle of a quagmire of monumental proportions. Words and elections have consequences. Trump voters remember this!

Americans, "Be not deceived; God is not mocked, for whatsoever a man soweth, that shall he also reap" (Galatians 6:7). Tweeting is not an effective way to establish governmental policy nor should it ever be. Executive Orders are procedurally a part of America's institutionalized governing processes, not TWEETING. Public Policies should be enacted utilizing the legislative process (elected officials). Tweeting is dictatorship and a potential tool of Communism, Nazism and Authoritarianism, not Social Democracy. As the ELECTED LEADER of the free-world tweeting established American domestic and foreign policies is simply what elephants leave on fairgrounds. In fact, tweeting is a personal pronoun disease called: "Me, Myself and I." And, the antidote is to stop tweeting American domestic and foreign policy initiatives, because the American governmental system is greater than "I, and I alone can fix it." The FIXER is GOD, not humans. Again, words and elections have both material as well as spiritual consequences.

Some naïve Americans who voted for Donald J. Trump state emphatically: "Give him a chance." However, the overwhelming majority of voters, almost 2.9 million, who did not vote for the Trumpster emphatically, say, give him a chance to do "WHAT"? Make America more White privilege (Nationalistic) oriented; institute religious and ethnic bigotry; make the rich, richer and the poor, poorer; make it more difficult for some to receive a college education; speed-up the process of climate change and environmental pollution; repeal Obamacare by changing the name while things remain the same, and spiritually demean women by referring to them as solely sexual-objects. Again, words and elections have both material as well as spiritual consequences.

Without a doubt, everything must change. Nothing remains the same. Or else HOPE is gone. In fact, the twenty-first century demands creative positive changes because of technological advances and robot-machines. Change means institutional reorientation. Above all, Christianity must reorient itself toward how we live in relationship with God and others; not Mega Church Construction. Christianity is about how you live, not how you die, because "For whatsoever is born of God overcometh the world: and this is the victory that overcometh the world, even our faith" (1 John 5: 4).

Therefore, change should create hope and justice for all, not societal confusion. Sometimes things only change because of the great equalizer, DEATH. "And as it is appointed unto men once to die, but after this the judgment" (Hebrews 9: 27). Without a doubt, every Christian Right Evangelical can shout this from Lookout Mountain in Tennessee, Stone Mountain in Georgia, and from the lowest elevation in Louisiana: "God judgeth the righteous, and God is angry with the wicked every day" (Psalms 7:11). Moreover, change should usher in the Kingdom of God on earth; whereby God's will is perfectly done as it is in heaven, not bring about moral confusion , and spiritual-mental warfare. For, all Christians know, "God is not the author of confusion, but peace, as in all churches of the saints" (1 Corinthians 14:33). Christian Right Evangelical pastors preach this scripture from your Mega-Churches.

The "Trump Administration" is not seeking to institute the will of God, but the "self-centered" will of the rich and powerful; as though the earth only belongs to them, not God (Psalms 24:1). This is precisely why President-elect Trump has surrounded himself with so many "super-wealthy" and "White Nationalists" cabinet appointees: Birds of a feather flock together.

The will of God is that we love one another; not build personal kingdoms or a WALL designed to keep the less fortunate (POOR) out. Humankind's loss of sacredness created an inability in individual humanity to perfect love, either vertically or horizontal, that is love for God or humankind. Moreover, the loss of sacredness created a desire in individuals to hear what they want to hear, and above all, interpret the meaning of what is said to fix their own selfish-narrative. But, most of all, loss of sacredness between God and humanity has thwarted man's spiritual ability to be what he is, but rather created in him an ungodly desire to be God. Individuals can become Christ-like, but not God. Stay in your lane as Christians, and live out the true meaning of the Two Great Commandments. Thanks to God, we have a Biblical-Spiritual Model for the tradition of divine love given to us by Jacob for loving your brother as well as your enemy. Selah!

CONCLUSION

Hatred is a deadly attitudinal disease that can not only destroy others, but one's self, as well. American society was built on self-defense, and hatred of Native Americans. But, through it all, every American should understand how good God has been to these United States of America. Above all, Americans should understand that: "There is no wisdom nor understanding nor counsel against the Lord" (Proverbs 21: 30).

Former President George W. Bush, through his family socialization, developed a spiritual moral conscience that informed his life concerning the spiritual-moral contradictions of American society. President Bush integrated his heart, mind, and soul with a tough Christian Faith, but a tender heart to love and serve others in Jesus' name.

In these perilous times of National ungodly greed, envy, jealousy, and unadulterated hatred for no cause; but just for the sake of it all, every American should spiritually understand that to hate another person for their skin tone is to hate God. God is the creator of everything. "Thou art worthy, O Lord, to receive glory and honour and power: for thou hast created all things, and for thy pleasure they are and were created" (Revelation 4:11). In his dedicatory speech President Bush reflected these inspirational spiritual principles.

And, at the dedication of the National Museum of African American History and Culture Former President George W. Bush said everything that needed to be said concerning America's spiritually troubling past, present and future. Thirteen years ago,

147

President George W. Bush authorized legislation to create the Museum, a bill that was authored by Representative John Lewis (D-Ga.) and Senator Samuel Brownback (R-Kan.) On Saturday, September 24th President Bush spoke these words of wisdom:

Thank you all. (To Laura). Thank you, darling. Laura has been very much engaged in this museum for a long time. She sits on the board. And we are honored to be here. My first reaction is I hope all of our fellow citizens come and look at this place. It is fabulous.

Mr. President and first lady, vice president, chief justice, Smithsonian Secretary David Skorton, thank you very much. The board. I do want to give a shout out to museum director Lonnie Bunch. It is really important to understand this project would not and could not have happened without his drive, his energy and his optimism.

As Laura mentioned, 15 years ago, members from both parties-Congressman John Lewis and Sam Brownback, then Senator from Kansas- informed me that they were about to introduce legislation creating a new museum to share the stories and celebrate the achievements of African Americans. You know, it would be fair to say that the congress and I did not always see eye to eye. If you know what I mean, Mr. President. But this is one issue where we strongly agreed. I was honored to sign the bill authorizing the construction of this national treasure. And I am pleased it now stands where it has always belonged, on the National Mall.

This museum is an important addition to our country for many reasons. Here are three. First, it shows our commitment to truth. A great nation does not hide its history. It faces its flaws and corrects them. This museum tells the truth that a country founded on the promise of liberty held millions in chains. That the price of our union was America's original sin. From the beginning, some spoke to truth. John Adams, who called slavery and "evil of colossal magnitude", their voices were not heeded, and often not heard. But they were always known to a power greater than any on earth, one who loves his children and meant them to be free.

Second, this museum shows America's capacity to change. For centuries, slavery and segregation seemed permanent. Permanent parts of our national life. But not to Nat Turner or Frederick Douglass; Harriet Tubman; Rosa Parks; or Martin Luther King, Jr. All answer cruelty with courage and hope.

In a society governed by the people, no wrong lasts forever. After struggle and sacrifice, the American people, acting through the most democratic means, amended the Constitution that originally treated slaves as three-fifths of a person, to guarantee equal protection of the laws. After a decade of struggle, civil rights acts and voting rights act were finally enacted. Even today, the journey toward justice is still not complete. But this museum will inspire us to go farther and get there faster.

And finally, the museum showcases the talent of some of our finest Americans. The galleries celebrate not only African American equality, but African American greatness. I cannot help but note that a huge influence in my teenage years is honored here, the great Chuck Berry. Or my baseball idol going up in far West Texas, the great Willie Mays. And of course, something that I never really mastered, the ability to give a good speech, but Thurgood Marshall sure could. And some of you may know I'm a fledgling painter, a struggle artist. I have a new appreciation for the artists whose brilliant works are displayed here, people like Robert Duncanson, Henry Ossawa Tanner, and Charles Henry Alston.

Our country is better and more vibrant because of their contributions and the contributions of millions of African Americans. No telling of American history is neither complete nor accurate without acknowledging them.

The lesson in this museum is that all Americans share a past and a future by staying true to our principles, righting injustice, and encouraging the empowerment of all. I congratulate all those who played a role in creating this wonderful museum. May God bless us all.

In conclusion every American should pray without ceasing that God helps us to spiritually overcome our Constitutional contradictions, as well as, our Christian shortcomings. Selah!